Battle
of
Antietam

by

Ted Ballard

Center of Military History
United States Army
Washington, D.C., 2008

Library of Congress Cataloging-in-Publication Data

Ballard, Ted.
    Battle of Antietam / by Ted Ballard.
        p. cm. — (Staff ride guide)
    1. Antietam, Battle of, Md., 1862. 2. Antietam National
Battlefield (Md.)—Guidebooks.   I. Title. II. Series.
    E474.65.B325 2006
    973.7'336—dc22

                                                                2006012153

Cover: Battle of Antietam, *Thure de Thulstrup*

First Printed 2006—CMH Pub 35–3–1

For sale by the Superintendent of Documents, U.S. Government Printing Office
Internet: bookstore.gpo.gov   Phone: toll free (866) 512-1800;   DC area (202) 512-1800
Fax: (202) 512-2104 Mail: Stop IDCC, Washington, DC 20402-0001

ISBN 978-0-16-081702-1

FOREWORD

The U.S. Army has long used the staff ride as a tool for professional development, conveying the lessons of the past to contemporary soldiers. In 1906 Maj. Eben Swift took twelve officer students from Fort Leavenworth's General Service and Staff School to the Chickamauga battlefield on the Army's first official staff ride. Since that time Army educators have employed the staff ride to provide Army officers with a better understanding of a past military operation, of the vagaries of war, and of military planning. It can also serve to enliven a unit's esprit de corps—a constant objective in peacetime or war.

To support the Army's initiatives, the Center is publishing staff ride guides such as this one on the Battle of Antietam. This account is drawn principally from contemporary and after-action reports, as well as from reminiscences of participants, both officers and enlisted men.

The Battle of Antietam provides important lessons in command and control, leadership, and unit training. This small volume should be a welcome training aid for those undertaking an Antietam staff ride and valuable reading for those interested in the Civil War and in the history of the military art.

Washington, D.C.   JOHN S. BROWN
15 September 2005   Brigadier General, USA (Ret.)
                                    Chief of Military History

THE AUTHOR

Ted Ballard was a historian with the U.S. Army Center of Military History from 1980–2004 and a part of the Center's staff ride program since 1986. *Battle of Antietam* joins his other battlefield guides to Ball's Bluff and First and Second Bull Run. He was a contributor to the Center's publication *The Story of the Noncommissioned Officer Corps;* the author of *Rhineland,* a brochure in the Center's series commemorating the fiftieth anniversary of World War II; and a contributor to the U.S. Army Training and Doctrine Command publication *American Military Heritage* and to the Virginia Army National Guard publication *The Tradition Continues: A History of the Virginia National Guard, 1607–1985.*

PREFACE

The Battle of Antietam has been called the bloodiest single day in American History. By the end of the evening, 17 September 1862, an estimated 4,000 American soldiers had been killed and over 18,000 wounded in and around the small farming community of Sharpsburg, Maryland. Emory Upton, then a captain with the Union artillery battery, later wrote, "I have heard of 'the dead lying in heaps,' but never saw it till this battle. Whole ranks fell together." The battle had been a day of confusion, tactical blunders, individual heroics, and the effects of just plain luck. It brought to an end a Confederate campaign to "liberate" the border state of Maryland and possibly to take the war into Pennsylvania. A little more than one hundred and forty years later, the Antietam battlefield is one of the best-preserved Civil War battlefields in the National Park System.

Antietam is ideal for a staff ride, since a continuing goal of the National Park Service is to maintain the site in the condition in which it was on the day of the battle. The purpose of any staff ride is to learn from the past by analyzing the battle through the eyes of the men who were there, both leaders and rank-and-file soldiers. Antietam offers many lessons in command and control, communications, intelligence, weapons technology versus tactics, and the ever-present confusion, or "fog" of battle. We hope that these lessons will allow us to gain insights into decision-making and the human condition during combat.

Several persons assisted in the creation of this staff ride guide. At the U.S. Army Center of Military History, Katherine Epstein edited the manuscript, Sherry Dowdy turned sketch maps into finished products, and Henrietta Snowden designed the final guide. Thanks also to Paul Chiles, Ted Alexander, Keith Snyder, and Brian Baracz, staff historians at the Antietam National Battlefield, who took time out from their busy schedules to review the manuscript for historical accuracy.

In the narrative, the names of Confederate personnel and units appear in italic type, Union personnel and units in regular type. Any errors that remain in the text are the sole responsibility of the author.

Washington, D.C.   TED BALLARD
4 May 2006

CONTENTS

Maps

Tables

Illustrations

Illustrations courtesy of the following: 93, National Portrait Gallery, Smithsonian Institution. All other illustrations from the Library of Congress.

Battle
of
Antietam

ANTIETAM: AN OVERVIEW

Prelude to the Battle

The year 1862 began with high hopes in Washington that the Confederate capital at Richmond, Virginia, would be captured and the war brought to a successful conclusion. A large, well-equipped force, the Army of the Potomac, had been organized and in the spring set out for the Union enclave at Fort Monroe, Virginia. Commanded by Maj. Gen. George B. McClellan, the Army of the Potomac then marched up the Virginia peninsula to lay siege to Richmond; other smaller commands remained in northern Virginia and the Shenandoah Valley to maintain security for the Federal capital.

However, instead of Union success, the spring and summer saw a string of Confederate victories in Virginia. In May and June a small Confederate force commanded by *Maj. Gen. Thomas J. "Stonewall" Jackson* separately defeated three small union commands in the Shenandoah Valley, threatening the security of Washington. To better defend the capital and possibly assist in the attack on Richmond, President Abraham Lincoln ordered that these three commands be consolidated into a force to be known as the Army of Virginia.

During the early summer, in the Seven Day's Battles, the Army of the Potomac was driven back from the Confederate capital by the Confederate *Army of Northern Virginia*, commanded by *General Robert E. Lee*. The Federal government then decided to withdraw the Army of the Potomac and join it with the Army of Virginia. However, before both Union commands could unite, *Lee*'s army marched north and in late August defeated the Army of Virginia at the Battle of Second Bull Run, thirty-five miles south of the Union capital. As summer came to an end, the Union had not captured Richmond and the Confederates appeared poised to capture Washington.

Although the year had seen one Confederate victory after another in Virginia, months of campaigning had taken its toll on the *Army of Northern Virginia*. *Lee's* command had suffered many casualties who would be difficult to replace. It was also short on rations and supplies, and literally thousands of *Lee's* troops were without sufficient clothing, especially shoes. As the *Army of Northern Virginia* prepared to embark on another major campaign, only its military organization prevented it from resembling a mob of hungry vagabonds.

In the days after Second Bull Run, the government in Washington prepared for an expected Confederate assault and *Lee* pondered his options. Insufficient numbers of troops, rations, ammunition, and other supplies prevented him from either attacking or engaging in a siege of the city. Washington was surrounded by extensive fortifications, bristling with artillery, and defended by large numbers of troops.

Lee could not afford to remain idle. It would be only a matter of time before Union forces reorganized and embarked on yet another advance into Virginia. To draw the Union Army out of its entrenchments around Washington and into the open, *Lee* planned to march north of Washington into Maryland. A Confederate movement north of the Potomac River would threaten both Washington and Baltimore and force the Federal government to devote large numbers of troops to defend those cities.

In early September *Lee* wrote to Confederate President *Jefferson Davis* that the *Army of Northern Virginia* was not properly equipped for such a campaign, especially since thousands of its men were barefoot. Nevertheless, *Lee* thought that his army was strong enough to keep the enemy occupied north of the Potomac until the approach of winter would make an enemy advance into Virginia difficult, if not impossible.[1] Richmond would be safe, at least until the following spring. On 4 September the *Army of Northern Virginia* crossed the Potomac River near Leesburg to the martial strains of "Maryland, My Maryland" and marched on to Frederick, Maryland.[2] (*Map 1*)

Fifty-five-year-old Virginian *Robert E. Lee* was the son of Revolutionary War hero General Henry "Light Horse Harry" Lee. *Robert E. Lee* graduated second in the West Point Class of 1829 and later served in the Mexican War, in which he was slightly wounded. He was superintendent of West Point from 1852 to 1855. In April 1861 *Lee* resigned his commission, hoping to remain out of the coming conflict. However, after Virginia seceded from the Union in late May, *Lee* accepted an appointment as commander of Virginia military forces. Later he served as military adviser to *Jefferson Davis*. On 1 June 1862, Davis assigned

---

[1] U.S. War Department, *The War of the Rebellion: A Compilation of the Official Records of the Union and Confederate Armies*, 70 vols. (Washington, D.C.: Government Printing Office, 1887), ser.1, vol. 19 (hereafter cited as OR), pt. 1, p. 144, and pt. 2, pp. 590–91.

[2] Henry Kyd Douglas, *I Rode with Stonewall* (Marietta, Ga.: R. Bemis Publishing, 1993), p. 620.

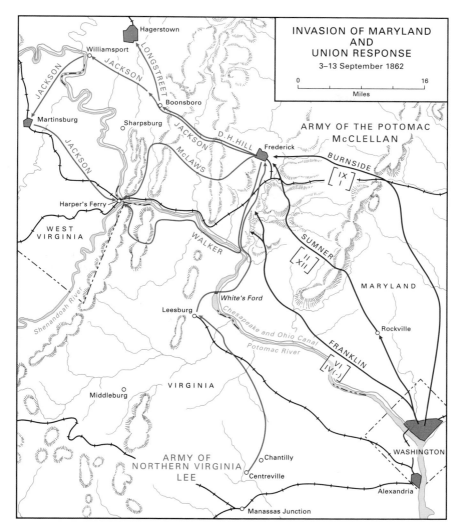

Map 1

Lee to command the force defending Richmond, which would soon become known as the *Army of Northern Virginia*. During the summer he led that army in the successful Battles of the Seven Days and Second Bull Run. Now, in early September, *Lee* led the *Army of Northern Virginia* north to the Potomac and into Maryland. He entered Maryland not on horseback but in an ambulance, for almost a week earlier he had fallen and broken a small bone in one hand and strained the other. His hands had

5

been placed in splints, with his right arm in a sling. It would be another week before he would be able to ride at all, and then only with a courier often leading his horse.[3]

At the beginning of the Maryland Campaign, the *Army of Northern Virginia* was organized into two infantry commands, or "wings."[4]

Forty-one-year-old *Maj. Gen. James Longstreet* commanded one wing of the army. A native of South Carolina, *Longstreet* had graduated from West Point in 1842. Like *Lee*, he was wounded in the Mexican War. At the beginning of the Civil War, *Longstreet* resigned his U.S. Army commission and accepted a commission as brigadier general in the Confederate Army, commanding an infantry division. In October of the same year *Longstreet* was appointed major general and during the summer of 1862 commanded a wing in the *Army of Northern Virginia*. *Longstreet*'s wing contained the divisions of *Maj. Gens. Lafayette McLaws* and *Richard H. Anderson*, as well as *Brig. Gens. David R. Jones, John B. Hood*, and *John G. Walker*.

Thirty-eight-year-old Virginian *Stonewall Jackson* commanded *Lee*'s other wing. *Jackson* had graduated from West Point in 1846 and resigned his commission almost ten years later to become an instructor at the Virginia Military Institute. When the Civil War broke out, *Jackson* accepted a colonelcy in the Virginia militia. Shortly thereafter, while a brigadier general at the First Battle of Bull Run, he earned the sobriquet Stonewall by standing firm against Union attacks. *Jackson*'s wing included the divisions of *Maj. Gen. Ambrose P. Hill, Maj. Gen. Daniel H. Hill* (*Jackson*'s brother-in-law), *Brig Gen. John R. Jones* commanding *Jackson*'s division, and *Brig. Gen. A. R. Lawton* commanding *Ewell*'s Division (the name given to the division previously commanded by *Maj. Gen. Richard S. Ewell*). *Jackson* also spent time traveling in an ambulance. Shortly after entering Maryland, he was injured when his horse reared up and fell on him. *Jackson* was severely bruised and unable to ride for several days.[5]

In addition to the two infantry wings, *Lee*'s army included a cavalry division commanded by 29-year-old *Maj. Gen. James E. B. Stuart*, a Virginian and 1854 graduate of West Point. *Stuart*'s division also included three batteries of artillery commanded by *Capt. John Pelham*.

The artillery of the *Army of Northern Virginia* at the Battle of Antietam totaled approximately 246 guns, at least 82 of which

---

[3] Ibid., p. 144. See also Robert E. Lee, *Recollections and Letters of Robert E. Lee* (New York: Garden City Publishing Co., Inc., 1904), pp. 78–79.

[4] These two commands were officially designated corps on 6 November.

[5] Douglas, *I Rode with Stonewall*, p. 620.

Previous to Antietam, *Alfred R. Waud. The drawing shows Confederates crossing the Potomac, with Union scouts in the foreground.*

were rifled, organized into batteries of 4–6 guns each. A battalion of several batteries was attached to each division, and four battalions of several batteries each were attached to the army's reserve artillery, command by *Brig. Gen. William N. Pendleton.*[6] The strength of the *Army of Northern Virginia* in July was almost 50,000 men. However, by the Battle of Antietam in mid-September, combat casualties, sickness, and straggling had reduced those numbers to roughly 35,000.[7]

After crossing the Potomac, the main portion of the *Army of Northern Virginia* reached Frederick by 7 September. The following day *Lee* issued a proclamation to the people of Maryland in which he promised "to aid you in throwing off this foreign yoke" and to restore sovereignty to the state.[8]

Meanwhile, the Federal government at Washington was moving to counter *Lee*'s advance into Maryland. On 5 September the Army of Virginia was officially consolidated with the Army of

---

[6] *OR*, pt.1, p. 835.

[7] Walter H. Taylor, *Four Years with General Lee* (Indianapolis: Indiana University Press, 1996), pp. 61, 73. See also *OR*, pt. 2, p. 602.

[8] *OR*, pt. 2, p. 602.

the Potomac, with the whole to be commanded by 35-year-old General McClellan. A West Point graduate of 1846 and former classmate of *General Jackson*'s, McClellan had resigned his commission in 1857. He served for a time with the Illinois Central Railroad and shortly before the Civil War was president of the eastern division of the Ohio and Mississippi Railroad. When war broke out, McClellan offered his services to the military forces of Ohio. In late 1861 he was summoned to Washington by President Lincoln, commissioned major general in the Regular Army, and appointed as general in chief of the Army.

Although McClellan was an excellent administrator and enormously popular with the troops, he was at constant odds with the Lincoln administration over military policy. In March 1862, when McClellan left Washington to accompany the Army of the Potomac to Fort Monroe, Lincoln relieved him as general in chief. (He retained command of the Army of the Potomac.) McClellan's continued bickering with the administration and the failure of his campaign before Richmond led to calls for his dismissal. It was, therefore, a surprise to many when Lincoln announced that McClellan would command the reorganized army during the Maryland Campaign. Lincoln believed that McClellan alone was capable of the complex task of quickly reorganizing and consolidating the two demoralized armies and then leading them immediately into battle. In addition to many regiments and batteries drawn from the defenses of Washington, the new elements of McClellan's army included the North Carolina Expeditionary Force of Maj. Gen. Ambrose E. Burnside's IX Corps. Burnside's command had arrived in northern Virginia in July from operations along the coast of the Carolinas. In early September Brig. Gen. Jacob D. Cox's Kanawha Division, which had arrived from western Virginia the previous month, was attached to the IX Corps.

When the War Department learned that *Lee*'s army had crossed into Maryland, McClellan was ordered to pursue immediately. By 7 September he was leading the Army of the Potomac north in search of *Lee*.

Lee, unaware of McClellan's pursuit, contemplated his next move at Frederick. He planned to shift his army westward across South Mountain to Hagerstown, Maryland, where he could establish a supply line to Winchester, Virginia, in the Shenandoah Valley. And, as *Lee* wrote *Davis*, "Should the results of the expedition justify it, I propose to enter Pennsylvania."[9] Aside from drawing the Union army farther from its base in Washington,

---

[9] Ibid., p. 592.

such a move would allow the Confederates to continue gathering much-needed supplies.

Blocking *Lee's* plan to open a line of communications into the Shenandoah Valley, however, were two Federal garrisons: 10,000 men at Harper's Ferry and about 2,000 at Martinsburg. *Lee* had expected both garrisons to flee westward after the Confederates crossed the Potomac, but instead authorities in Washington had ordered the garrisons to remain in place. Their presence meant that *Lee* would have to capture the enemy garrisons before continuing his march toward Pennsylvania. In a discussion with *Longstreet*, *Lee* proposed dividing the army into several elements to accomplish the mission. *Longstreet* advised against such a move, arguing that the Union army at Washington, though disorganized and demoralized after Second Bull Run, was still a threat. He said that he knew a number of Union commanders who could "put it in order and march against us, if they found us exposed, and make a serious trouble before the capture [of Harper's Ferry] could be accomplished." *Lee* spoke no more of the proposal to *Longstreet*, who thought the plan "a mere passing thought."

However, *Longstreet's* assessment was premature. *Lee*, after consultation with *Jackson*, decided to capture the two garrisons.[10] On 9 September *Lee* issued Special Orders 191,[11] which explained the Harper's Ferry operation in detail, including the routes of march for the various units involved. (*See Map 2.*) *Jackson*, with the divisions commanded by *J. R. Jones*, *Lawton*, and *A. P. Hill*, was to recross the Potomac River at Williamsport, Maryland, and capture the garrison at Martinsburg. *Jackson* and his command were then to march to Harper's Ferry, approaching the town from the west. *Longstreet's* divisions under *McLaws*, *R. H. Anderson*, and *Walker* would assist *Jackson* at Harper's Ferry. *McLaws* and *Anderson* were to march directly to Harper's Ferry and occupy the heights north of the Potomac and east of the town, while *Walker* was to cross the Potomac at Point of Rocks and occupy the heights south of the town. While *Stuart's* cavalry screened the army's various movements, the division of *D. H. Hill* was to occupy Boonsboro to prevent any Union troops in Harper's Ferry from escaping in that direction. Although the order indicated that *Longstreet's* command was to halt at Boonsboro, *Longstreet*, along with *Lee* and the divisions of *D. R. Jones* and *Hood*, continued on to Hagerstown. The division of *D. H. Hill* was to halt at Boonsboro as a rear guard. At the successful

---

[10] James Longstreet, *From Manassas to Appomattox* (Philadelphia: J. B. Lippincott Co., 1896), pp. 201–02.

[11] *OR*, pt. 2, pp. 603–04.

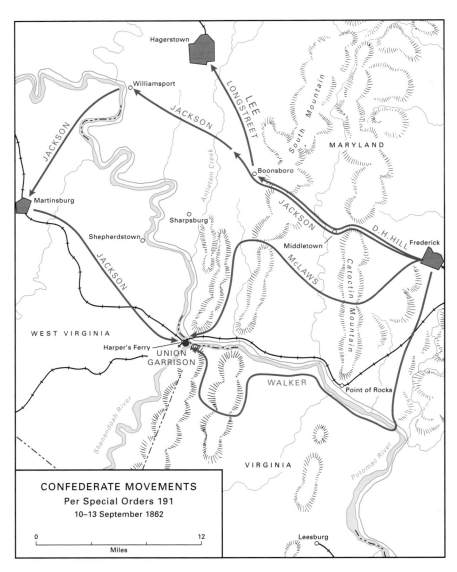

Map 2

conclusion of the operation, *Lee's* army was to reunite at Hagerstown; at that time he would determine whether to continue to march north into Pennsylvania. Despite *Longstreet's* forebodings about the operation, *Lee* was certain that McClellan would remain for some time near Washington to complete the Union

Army's reorganization. *Lee* also expected the Harper's Ferry operation to be completed no later than 13 September.[12]

The Confederate army departed Frederick on 10 September. *Jackson*'s command marched to Williamsport, where it forded the Potomac while bands played "Carry Me Back to Ole Virginny."[13] On 12 September, as *Jackson* approached Martinsburg, the Federal garrison there fled to Harper's Ferry. The following morning *Jackson* resumed his march; by the evening of 13 September, the time by which *Lee* had hoped the operation would be finished, the commands of *Jackson*, *Walker*, *R. H. Anderson*, and *McLaws* were surrounding Harper's Ferry.

On 12 September, only two days after the Confederate army's departure from Frederick, elements of the Army of the Potomac began entering that city. The following day McClellan himself arrived. The 80,000-man Union army was organized into three wings. Thirty-eight-year-old General Burnside commanded the army's right wing, consisting of the I Corps, led by Maj. Gen. Joseph Hooker, and the IX Corps, led by Maj. Gen. Jesse L. Reno. Sixty-five-year-old Maj. Gen. Edwin V. Sumner commanded the center wing, which included Sumner's own II Corps and the XII Corps, commanded by Maj. Gen. Nathaniel Banks. Because Banks had been retained in Washington to command the defense of the capital, the corps was placed under the temporary command of Maj. Gen. Joseph K. F. Mansfield. Thirty-nine-year-old Maj. Gen. William B. Franklin commanded McClellan's left wing, which included Franklin's own VI Corps and the division of Maj. Gen. Darius Couch. Couch's division had been part of the IV Corps, but that organization had recently been disbanded and Couch's division attached to Franklin's command. Brig. Gen. Alfred Pleasonton commanded McClellan's cavalry division, which contained five brigades of cavalry. McClellan's field artillery consisted of approximately 300 guns, typically organized into batteries of 6 guns, each with several batteries assigned to each division. Almost 60 percent of McClellan's artillery was rifled.

After McClellan arrived at Frederick on the morning of 13 September, circumstances intervened on his behalf. That morning a Union enlisted man camping near town found several cigars around which was wrapped a copy of *Lee*'s Special Orders 191, which had been lost by a Confederate courier.[14] By early afternoon the document was in McClellan's hands.

---

[12] Longstreet, *From Manassas to Appomattox*, p. 206.

[13] Douglas, *I Rode with Stonewall*, p. 623.

[14] Silas Colgrove, "The Finding of Lee's Lost Order," in *Battles and Leaders of the Civil War*, ed. Robert U. Johnson and Clarence C. Buel, 4 vols. (New York: The Century Co., 1887) (hereafter cited as *B&L*), 2: 603.

McClellan now knew of *Lee*'s plan for the capture of Harper's Ferry and of the division of the Confederate army into several smaller commands. If McClellan moved quickly, he could cross South Mountain, interpose his army between *Lee*'s forces, and defeat them one at a time. McClellan later wrote that he "immediately gave orders for a rapid and vigorous forward movement."[15] But the pursuit did not occur that afternoon. Earlier in the day the IX Corps had been sent to cross Catoctin Mountain and was approaching Middletown. McClellan ordered the IX Corps to continue to Turner's and Fox's Gaps on South Mountain the following morning. At 1820 McClellan also ordered the VI Corps to cross Crampton's Gap the following morning. Around midnight a confident McClellan sent a telegram to President Lincoln: "I have all the plans of the rebels, and will catch them in their own trap if my men are equal to the emergency." He added, "Will send you trophies."[16]

McClellan's confidence about confronting *Lee*'s army, however, came to be tempered by his mistaken belief that *Lee*'s army outnumbered him. From a variety of sources, he was getting estimates of Confederate strength ranging from 80,000–200,000 men.[17] Moreover, as McClellan telegraphed Washington, "Everything seems to indicate that they intend to hazard all upon the issue of the coming battle. They are probably aware that their forces are numerically superior to ours by at least 25 per cent."[18] Observing that a general battle against such odds "might, to say the least, be doubtful," McClellan asked to be reinforced by troops stationed in defense of Washington. The administration responded by sending the V Corps, commanded by Maj. Gen. Fitz John Porter.

On the evening of 13 September *Lee* received the unwelcome news from *Stuart*'s cavalry scouts that the Union army had reached Frederick. *Stuart* estimated Union strength to be 90,000.[19] Shortly afterward *Lee* may have learned from *Stuart* that, according to a local citizen, a copy of Special Orders 191 was in McClellan's hands.[20] With McClellan aware of *Lee*'s scattered forces and the Union army approaching the South Mountain

---

[15] George B. McClellan, *McClellan's Own Story* (New York: Charles L. Webster and Co., 1887), p. 572.

[16] *OR*, pt. 2, p. 281.

[17] Ibid., pp. 233, 248.

[18] Ibid., p. 254.

[19] Longstreet, *From Manassas to Appomattox*, p. 219.

[20] Joseph L. Harsh, *Sounding the Shallows: A Confederate Companion for the Maryland Campaign of 1862* (Kent, Ohio: Kent State University Press, 2000), pp. 170–71.

gaps, *Lee* had to act quickly. He ordered *D. H. Hill*, supported by *Hood* and *D. R. Jones*, to defend Turner's and Fox's Gaps. Farther south, *McLaws* was to continue his role in the Harper's Ferry operation but send a part of his force to defend Crampton's Gap.

On 14 September McClellan's right wing, commanded by Burnside and consisting of Hooker's I Corps and Reno's IX Corps, fought its way to the top of South Mountain. (*See Map 3.*) By evening the Confederate defenders barely held their ground on the crest. During the fighting Reno was killed, and General Cox assumed command of the IX Corps. Six miles to the south, Franklin's VI Corps attacked Crampton's Gap. After a hard-fought battle with *McLaws'* defenders, Union forces occupied the gap. It had taken all day, but McClellan's army had captured one mountain gap and would probably force its way through the other two the following morning. McClellan was jubilant. He telegraphed the War Department, "It had been a glorious victory." When the results of the Battles of South Mountain reached the White House, Lincoln, who only a few days earlier had feared a Confederate attack on Washington, telegraphed McClellan: "Your dispatch of to-day received. God bless you and all with you! Destroy the rebel army, if possible."[21]

Having watched the defense of the northern gaps, late in the evening *Lee* determined that the troops at hand were insufficient to prevent an expected Union attempt to cross the mountain the following morning. Consequently, he decided to end the campaign in Maryland and withdraw the troops then with him to Virginia by way of a Potomac River ford at Shepherdstown. But shortly thereafter *Lee* received the news that Union troops had taken Crampton's Gap. If the Union troops crossed through that gap the following morning, they could relieve the Union garrison at Harper's Ferry. To guard against the potential Union maneuver, *Lee* decided to halt his retreat near Sharpsburg and threaten any enemy force moving against *McLaws'* and *Anderson's* rear.

On the morning of 15 September *Lee*, along with *Longstreet*, *D. R. Jones'* and *D. H. Hill's* divisions, and a portion of *Stuart's* cavalry, reached Sharpsburg on Boonsboro Pike. The town is just east of Antietam Creek and only about three miles from the Potomac River. A bridge across the river had been destroyed earlier in the war, but the river could be crossed at Boteler's Ford, less than a mile downstream from Shepherdstown.

Around noon *Lee* received news of the surrender of the Harper's Ferry garrison. The surrender was announced to the

---

[21] McClellan, *McClellan's Own Story*, p. 583.

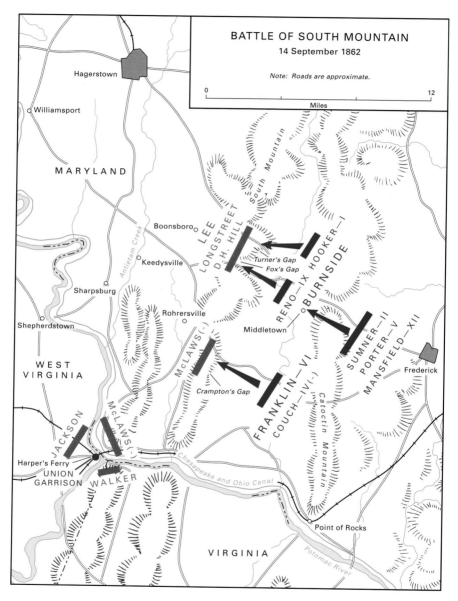

BATTLE OF SOUTH MOUNTAIN
14 September 1862

Note: Roads are approximate.

0   12
                        Miles

Hagerstown

Williamsport

MARYLAND

Boonsboro

Keedysville

Antietam Creek

Sharpsburg

Rohrersville

Shepherdstown

Middletown

WEST
VIRGINIA

Harper's Ferry
UNION
GARRISON

Chesapeake and Ohio Canal

WALKER

Point of Rocks

VIRGINIA

Potomac River

LEE
LONGSTREET
D.H. HILL
South Mountain
Turner's Gap
Fox's Gap
RENO—IX
HOOKER—I
BURNSIDE

McLAWS(—)
Crampton's Gap

FRANKLIN—VI
COUCH—IV(—)
Catoctin Mountain

SUMNER—II
PORTER—V
MANSFIELD—XII
Frederick

JACKSON
McLAWS(—)

Map 3

army, which, according to *Lee*, "reanimated the courage of the troops."[22] A short time later *Stuart* arrived to inform *Lee* of the large number of Union prisoners captured at Harper's Ferry and the vast amounts of supplies. With thousands of his men barefoot, *Lee* quickly responded, "General, did they have any shoes?" Pointing to a Confederate unit standing barefoot nearby, *Lee* told *Stuart*, "These good men need shoes."[23]

With Harper's Ferry captured and the Confederate victors now marching to rejoin the army at Sharpsburg, *Lee* elected to remain in Maryland a little longer. *Lee* made a risky decision to remain north of the Potomac River and confront an enemy he believed to outnumber his army by two to one. On 15 September *Lee* had on hand at Sharpsburg only about 25,000 men. The Confederates at Harper's Ferry might add another 15,000 men, but it would be a day at least before these troops might rejoin the army at Sharpsburg. At *Lee*'s back was the Potomac River. If *Lee* was driven back to Boteler's Ford by an aggressive enemy, it might mean disaster for the Confederates. Still, *Lee* was reluctant to withdraw from Maryland so soon after his "liberating" entry only a week earlier. And even though his command might be outnumbered, he had confidence that his men could hold their own against the Army of the Potomac. He decided to make a stand at Sharpsburg.

In 1862 three narrow stone bridges crossed Antietam Creek in the vicinity of Sharpsburg. A road from Keedysville on Boonsboro Pike crossed the stream at the northernmost, or upper, bridge near the mill of Philip Pry. A mile south of the upper bridge, Boonsboro Pike crossed over the middle bridge (now replaced by a modern highway bridge). A mile south of Sharpsburg, the lower bridge, now called Burnside Bridge, crossed the stream. Antietam Creek could also be crossed at Pry's Mill Ford, a half-mile south of the upper bridge; at Snavely's Ford, a mile south of the lower bridge; and at several other smaller farm fords.

Lee deployed his small command around Sharpsburg. (*See Map 4.*) The division of *D. R. Jones* was placed on high ground east of the town and south of Boonsboro Pike. The small brigade of *Brig. Gen. Robert Toombs* was assigned to guard the lower bridge. Farther south, a portion of *Stuart's* cavalry guarded the army's right flank. Northeast of town, *D. H. Hill's* division was placed

---

[22] Clifford Dowdey, ed., *The Wartime Papers of Robert E. Lee* (Boston: Little, Brown and Co., 1961), p. 318.
[23] Ezar A. Carman, Unpubl Narrative History of the Battle, copy on file at Antietam National Battlefield, ch. 9, p. 55.

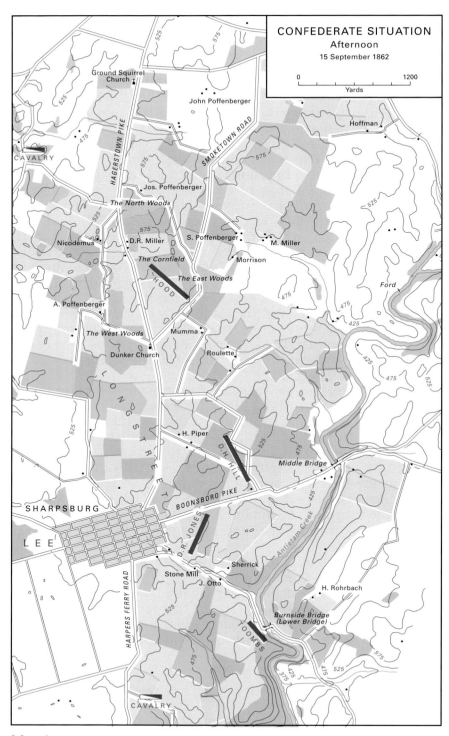

CONFEDERATE SITUATION
Afternoon
15 September 1862

0   1200
Yards

Ground Squirrel Church
John Poffenberger
Hoffman
CAVALRY
Jos. Poffenberger
The North Woods
Nicodemus
D.R. Miller
S. Poffenberger
M. Miller
Morrison
The Cornfield
The East Woods
Ford
A. Poffenberger
The West Woods
Mumma
Roulette
Dunker Church
H. Piper
Middle Bridge
SHARPSBURG
BOONSBORO PIKE
LEE
D. R. JONES
Sherrick
Stone Mill
J. Otto
H. Rohrbach
Burnside Bridge
(Lower Bridge)
TOOMBS
CAVALRY

HAGERSTOWN PIKE
SMOKETOWN ROAD
HOOD
LONGSTREET
D. H. HILL
HARPERS FERRY ROAD
Antietam Creek

Map 4

between the middle bridge and Dunker Church. (Also known as Dunkard Church, the small white structure belonged to a pacifist sect known as the Church of the Brethren. Outsiders called the congregation Dunkers or Dunkards because of a doctrine of three total immersions during baptism.) *Hood*'s division was placed near Dunker Church. Surrounding *Hood*'s command were three woodlots known as the West, North, and East Woods and a gently rolling farmland of cornfields, plowed fields, and pastures. On the opposite side of the pike from the church almost half a mile farther north was a thirty-acre cornfield that would gain notoriety in the battle. To guard the army's left flank, another portion of *Stuart*'s cavalry was placed northwest of Dunker Church near the bend in the Potomac River. *Lee* established his headquarters in a tent on the western edge of town on Boonsboro Pike.

McClellan's army began crossing the northern gaps of South Mountain on the morning of 15 September and marched toward Sharpsburg. To the south, Franklin's VI Corps, followed by Couch's division, crossed at Crampton's Gap. Franklin's mission had been to relieve the Harper's Ferry garrison; but some time after noon the mission changed when, as McClellan later wrote, "the total cessation of firing in the direction of Harper's Ferry indicated but too clearly the shameful and premature surrender of the post."[24] McClellan ordered Franklin and Couch to halt at the western foot of South Mountain and await further orders.

McClellan's army began arriving on the east side of Antietam Creek on the afternoon of 15 September. Although a force of Confederates could be seen halted on the west side of the creek, McClellan believed that the enemy was in full retreat and would cross the Potomac River back into Virginia that night.[25] McClellan established his headquarters on Boonsboro Pike about a mile south of Keedysville. While the cavalry halted on the heights east of the middle bridge, Maj. Gen. Israel B. Richardson's and Brig. Gen. George Sykes' divisions took positions opposite the bridge and Hooker's I Corps halted east of the upper bridge. Sumner, with Maj. Gen. John Sedgwick's and Brig. Gen. William French's divisions and Mansfield's XII Corps, halted at Keedysville. McClellan later said that he had hoped to make an attack that afternoon; but "after a rapid examination of the position, I found it was too late to attack that day."[26] Instead, he spent the afternoon waiting for more troops to arrive, assigning positions for the troops to camp that night, and placing artillery batteries,

[24] *OR*, pt. 1, p. 29.
[25] Carman, Unpubl Narrative History, ch. 13, p. 5.
[26] *OR*, pt. 1, p. 29.

including long-range rifled artillery, on the ridge overlooking the creek. That evening Cox's IX Corps arrived and was placed opposite the lower bridge. During the day McClellan had suspended the organization of Burnside's right wing and ordered Hooker to report directly to him rather than to Burnside.[27] Burnside was assigned command of the left wing of the army, which consisted of only the IX Corps.

On the morning of 16 September McClellan, still expecting the Confederates to be mostly across the river in Virginia, wrote to his wife: "Have reached thus far and have no doubt delivered Penna and Maryland. All well and in excellent spirits."[28] McClellan also sent a telegram to Washington: "This morning a heavy fog has thus far prevented our doing more than to ascertain that some of the enemy are still there. Do not yet know in what force. Will attack as soon as situation of the enemy is developed."[29] When the fog cleared, McClellan spent most of the morning riding along his line, "examining the ground, finding fords, clearing approaches, and hurrying up ammunition and supply-trains."[30] Around noon Maj. Gen. George W. Morell's division of the V Corps arrived, accompanied by Porter himself, and was halted near Keedysville.

While McClellan continued to prepare to attack, *Jackson* and the divisions of *J. R. Jones* and *Lawton* arrived at Sharpsburg, rejoining *Jackson's* third division, commanded by *D. H. Hill*. *Jackson's* fourth division, that of *A. P. Hill*, remained at Harper's Ferry to secure captured property and parole the large number of prisoners (about 12,000). *Walker's* division of *Longstreet's* command also arrived from Harper's Ferry and halted a short distance south of the town.

By 1330 McClellan was finally ready to go on the offensive, but he was reluctant to commit a large portion of his army to a frontal attack. Instead, he ordered Hooker's I Corps, stationed by the upper bridge, to cross Antietam Creek and if possible to turn *Lee's* left flank. McClellan later started in his report of the battle:

> My plan for the impending engagement was to attack the enemy's left with the corps of Hooker and Mansfield, supported by Sumner's and, if necessary, by Franklin's; and as matters look favorably there, to move the corps of Burnside against the enemy's extreme right, upon the ridge running to the south and rear of Sharpsburg, and having

---

[27] Ibid. See also p. 418.
[28] Stephen W. Sears, ed., *The Civil War Papers of George B. McClellan: Selected Correspondence*, 1860–1865 (New York: Ticknor and Fields, 1989), p. 566.
[29] OR, pp. 307–08.
[30] McClellan, *McClellan's Own Story*, p. 590.

The Lower, or Burnside, Bridge from the Union Side

carried their position, to press along the crest towards our right; and whenever either of these flank movements should be successful, to advance our center with all the forces then disposable.[31]

However, if McClellan had indeed formulated such a plan before the battle, he apparently failed to impart it to Hooker, who was under the impression that the I Corps with roughly 8,500 men was acting alone. Hooker's corps consisted of three divisions commanded by Brig. Gens. Abner Doubleday, James B. Ricketts, and George G. Meade. It was not until approximately 1530 or 1600 that the divisions of Meade and Ricketts crossed at the upper bridge and began marching toward Hagerstown Pike while Doubleday's division crossed nearby Pry's Mill Ford. (*See Map 5.*)

Hooker's command had not gone much over half a mile when Hooker began to have doubts about attacking the Confederates with only his corps. Hooker informed McClellan that if he were not reinforced, or unless a simultaneous attack was made on the Confederate right flank, "the rebels would eat me up."[32] McClellan promised reinforcements and ordered Sumner's XII Corps, commanded by Mansfield, from Keedysville to support Hooker. Sumner was also to be prepared to send the II Corps from Keedysville for the same purpose the next morning. To be closer to the impending action, McClellan moved his headquarters to the home of Philip Pry, about half a mile south of the upper bridge, just west of Boonsboro Pike.

Lee, Longstreet, and *Jackson* were meeting in the center of Sharpsburg when a courier brought word that Union troops were crossing Antietam at the upper bridge. Around the same time they also received news of enemy movements near the

---

[31] Ibid.
[32] Ibid., p. 217.

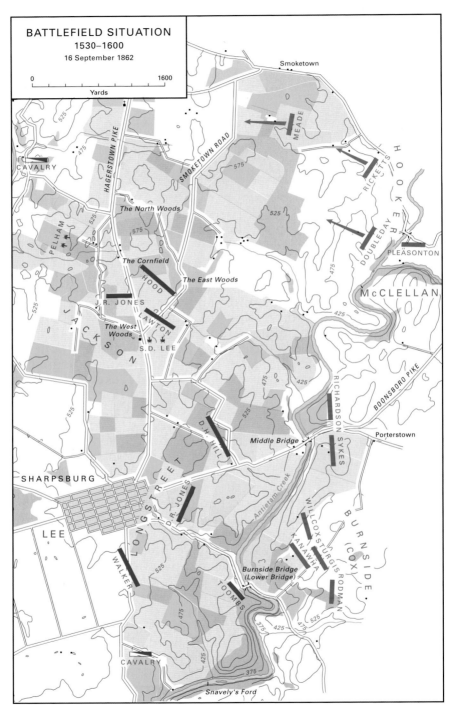

BATTLEFIELD SITUATION
1530–1600
16 September 1862

0   1600

Yards

Smoketown

CAVALRY

HAGERSTOWN PIKE

SMOKETOWN ROAD

MEADE

HOOKER

RICKETTS

PELHAM

The North Woods

DOUBLEDAY

PLEASONTON

The Cornfield

HOOD

The East Woods

J. R. JONES

JACKSON

LAWTON

The West Woods

S. D. LEE

McCLELLAN

RICHARDSON

SYKES

BOONSBORO PIKE

D. H. HILL

Middle Bridge

Porterstown

SHARPSBURG

LONGSTREET

D. R. JONES

Antietam Creek

WILLCOX

STURGIS

KANAWHA

BURNSIDE
(COX)

LEE

RODMAN

WALKER

TOOMBS

Burnside Bridge
(Lower Bridge)

CAVALRY

Snavely's Ford

Map 5

Burnside Bridge, a Confederate View

lower bridge. To meet the northern threat, *Lee* sent *Jackson* with
J. R. Jones' command toward Dunker Church to join with *Hood*.
Lawton was initially ordered to support *Toombs'* brigade at the
lower bridge; but after *Lee* determined that there was no Union
attempt to cross the lower bridge, *Lawton* was sent to join *Jackson*. *Walker's* command remained south of Sharpsburg, available
to support *Toombs* if necessary.

Shortly before dark Hooker's columns, preceded by skirmishers from Meade's division, reached the East Woods. *Hood's* division opened a lively skirmish with Meade's men, but darkness
and a drizzling rain ended the confrontation. *Hood* then withdrew to the West Woods, south of Dunker Church. *Jackson* extracted a promise from *Hood* that his division would return to
the front the moment it was called upon.

Leaving Brig. Gen. Truman Seymour's brigade of Meade's
division in the East Woods, the remainder of Hooker's corps
moved into bivouac just east of Hagerstown Pike and north
of the Joseph Poffenberger home. Hooker, still nervous about
confronting an enemy that he believed to outnumber him, informed McClellan that his attack would begin at dawn. He also
asked that reinforcements be sent to him before the attack.

During the night McClellan ordered Franklin's VI Corps,
still near Crampton's Gap, to join the main army at Sharpsburg.
Couch's division was ordered to remain in place. Around midnight, per McClellan's orders, the 7,500-man XII Corps crossed
Antietam Creek and by 0200 encamped about two miles north
of the East Woods, joining Hooker's I Corps.

Facing the threat of an attack the following morning, *Lee*
ordered *A. P. Hill's* division at Harper's Ferry to march for Sharpsburg at first light. *Hill* was to leave a small force behind to complete the removal of captured property.

Shortly before daylight on 17 September Hooker's corps began to stir, initiating heavy firing between the pickets of both sides. By roughly 0600 the rain had ceased, and the I Corps began its advance south through a low-lying morning mist. (*Map 6*) Hooker stated that this immediate objective was to reach high ground almost a mile to the south (site of the present-day Visitor Center).[33] While Doubleday's division marched south along Hagerstown Pike, Ricketts' division moved west of Smoketown Road. The brigades of Col. Albert L. Magilton and Lt. Col. Robert Anderson of Meade's division waited in reserve near the North Woods. Seymour's brigade, also of Meade's division, remained in an advanced position in the southwest corner of the East Woods. In addition to Hooker's own artillery placed on high ground near the Joseph Poffenberger farm, his advance was also supported by long-range rifled guns on the heights east of Antietam Creek. These guns enfiladed *Jackson*'s lines, dropping rounds randomly along Hagerstown Pike.

Under heavy fire from Union artillery, *Jackson*'s command waited. The division of *J. R. Jones* was west of Hagerstown Pike, about 500 yards north of Dunker Church. Farther west, the brigade of *Brig. Gen. Jubal A. Early*, part of *Lawton*'s division, supported *Stuart*'s cavalry. East of the pike, on the southern edge of the Cornfield, *Lawton* extended *Jackson*'s line toward the East Woods. South of this position, near the home of Samuel Mumma, a portion of *Lawton*'s command protected *Jackson*'s right flank.

While Union artillery kept up a steady fire into *Jackson*'s position, Confederate guns quickly responded. Along Nicodemus Hill, fourteen guns of *Pelham*'s artillery opened fire into Brig. Gen. John Gibbon's brigade of Doubleday's division. One of *Hood*'s artillery battalions, commanded by *Col. Stephen D. Lee* and directly in the path of the Union advance, fired from a knoll just east of Hagerstown Pike and opposite Dunker Church. As the gunners on both sides kept up a lively fire, a civilian spectator noted, "The cannonade, reverberating from cloud to mountain and from mountain to cloud, became a continuous roar, like the unbroken roll of a thunder-storm."[34]

Jackson's men did not have long to wait. Doubleday's and Ricketts' divisions soon reached the Miller farm and halted north of the Cornfield. The corn stood six feet high, but Hooker

---

[33] Ibid., p. 218.
[34] Charles C. Coffin, "Antietam Scenes," in *B&L*, p. 682.

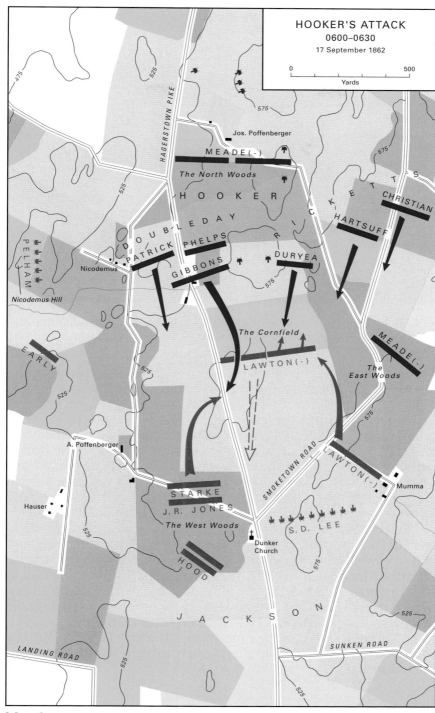

Map 6

Battle of Antietam, *Thure de Thulstrup, Showing the Union Advance on the Dunker Church*

deduced from the bayonets protruding above the corn that the field contained a large number of Confederate troops. Hooker ordered two batteries of artillery forward from the Joseph Poffenberger farm, and the guns began raking the Cornfield with round after round of canister. Hooker vividly described the scene: "In the time I am writing every stalk of corn in the northern and greater part of the field was cut as closely as could have been done with a knife, and the slain lay in rows precisely as they stood in their ranks a few moments before. It was never my fortune to witness a more bloody, dismal battle-field."[35]

Shortly afterward, the infantry advance resumed. As Ricketts' division approached the Cornfield, two of his three brigades halted when the commander of one was seriously wounded and the other lost his nerve. The result was that only one of Ricketts' brigades entered the Cornfield to confront *Lawton*'s division. After a short but bitter standup fight, the Union brigade was driven back with heavy losses. Ricketts' remaining two brigades, now under new commanders, attacked *Lawton*; but the assaults were uncoordinated and each in turn was driven from the Cornfield.

---

[35] *OR*, pt. 1, p. 218.

Confederate Dead along the West Side of Hagerstown Pike. The Cornfield is to the right.

While Ricketts' brigades fought in the eastern portion of the Cornfield, Doubleday's division fought in the western portion. An officer in Doubleday's command afterward wrote, "Men, I cannot say fell; they were knocked out of the ranks by dozens."[36] Near Hagerstown Pike, Doubleday's men struck the left of *Lawton's* command and drove the Confederates back. A portion of *J. R. Jones'* division then attacked Doubleday, but it was driven back. After losing many casualties, *Lawton's* command also fell back to join *D. R. Jones*. The bloody Cornfield was in Union hands.

By 0700 over half of *Jackson's* command had been killed or wounded. *J. R. Jones* left the field after being stunned by the explosion of artillery shell. *Brig. Gen. William E. Starke*, a brigade commander in Jones' command, was killed, the first Confederate general to be killed or mortally wounded during the battle. With his line collapsing, *Jackson* called on *Hood's* division for assistance.

Hood's men were preparing breakfast in the West Woods southwest of Dunker Church when they received orders to move

---

[36] Rufus R. Dawes, *Service with the Sixth Wisconsin Volunteers* (Marietta, Ga.: E. R. Alderman and Sons, 1890), p. 90.

at once to the front. The command quickly departed the woods and headed north with *Col. William T. Wofford's* brigade on the left and *Col. Evander M. Law's* brigade on the right. (*Map 7*) Doubleday's and Ricketts' divisions had resumed their advance when they were suddenly attacked by *Hood's* men. A Union Officer remembered, "A long and steady gray line, unbroken by the fugitives who fly before us, comes sweeping down through the woods around the church. They raise the yell and fire. It is like a scythe running through our line. 'Now save, who can.' It is a race for life that each man runs for the cornfield."[37]

The left of *Hood's* division drove into the Cornfield, where another round of violence exploded. *Hood* later wrote, "It was here that I witnessed the most terrible clash of arms, by far, that has occurred during the war."[38] As his men pressed forward, *Hood's* left flank came under fire from Doubleday's troops, who had fallen back to the west side of Hagerstown Pike. Battery B, 4th U.S. Artillery, also west of the pike, opened fire on the Confederates. The guns fired canister at a range of less than twenty-five yards, throwing splintered pieces of fence rails and men alike into the air. The Confederates who survived the blast began shooting down the gunners.

While part of *Hood's* command fought along the pike, the *1st Texas Infantry* pushed through the Cornfield toward the Miller farmhouse, where Magilton's and Anderson's brigades of Meade's division had arrived earlier. The one-sided confrontation resulted in the Texans' suffering over 80 percent casualties and retreating to the Cornfield.

Meanwhile, the right of *Hood's* division entered the East Woods. There, it confronted Mansfield's newly arrived XII Corps, which McClellan had ordered to support Hooker the day before. Mansfield, thinking that his command was firing on Hooker's men, rode in front of his line to halt the firing and was mortally wounded. Brig. Gen. Alpheus S. Williams, one of Mansfield's division commanders, assumed command of the corps and launched a counterattack into the Cornfield. *Hood's* command was driven back to the West Woods.

While Williams' division halted in the Cornfield, the other division of the XII Corps, commanded by Brig. Gen. George S. Greene, detached one brigade to support Williams. Greene's two remaining brigades continued south on Smoketown Road. *Colonel Lee's* guns quickly withdrew, and Greene halted on a plateau east of Dunker Church. It was around this time that Hooker received a slight wound in the foot and turned over command

---

[37] Ibid.
[38] *OR*, pt. 1, p. 923.

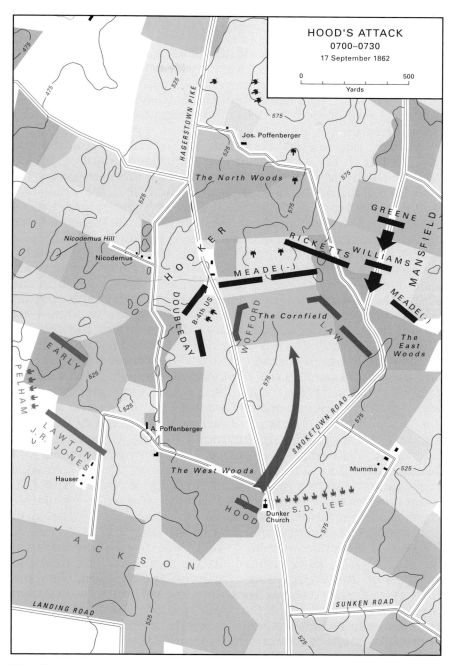

HOOD'S ATTACK
0700–0730
17 September 1862

0   500
Yards

HAGERSTOWN PIKE

Jos. Poffenberger

The North Woods

GREENE

Nicodemus Hill

Nicodemus

HOOKER

RICKETTS

WILLIAMS

MANSFIELD

MEADE(-)

MEADE(-)

DOUBLEDAY

B.4th US

WOFFORD

The Cornfield

LAW

The
East
Woods

EARLY

PELHAM

LAWTON

J.R. JONES

A. Poffenberger

SMOKETOWN ROAD

Mumma

Hauser

The West Woods

HOOD

Dunker
Church

S.D. LEE

JACKSON

LANDING ROAD

SUNKEN ROAD

Map 7

of the I Corps to Meade. Meade, believing that the XII Corps was arriving to relieve Hooker's corps, began withdrawing the I Corps toward the North Woods.

As the fighting momentarily paused, McClellan ordered Sumner to send two of his three divisions to support Hooker. Sumner led Sedgwick's and French's divisions across the creek at Pry's Mill Ford and headed for the battlefield. Sumner's third division, commanded by Richardson, remained east of the creek guarding artillery.

Shortly before 0900 Sumner's two divisions reached the East Woods. After a brief halt, the command resumed its advance, which did not progress in a unified manner. (*Map 8*) It split first around Greene's division, which held the open plateau near Dunker Church, with Sedgwick's three brigades moving to Greene's right into the West Woods and French's three brigades moving to Greene's left. Then, within the advance of Sedgwick's division on the West Woods, one of Brig. Gen. Willis A. Gorman's regiments, the 34th New York Infantry, became detached and ended up near Dunker Church. There, it found the 125th Pennsylvania Infantry, which had become separated from Williams' division and had entered the West Woods some time earlier. Thus, Sumner's two divisions did not attack together.

Sumner personally led Sedgwick's division to Hagerstown Pike, where the men climbed post-and-rail fences on either side of the road and entered the West Woods. Sedgwick's leading brigade, commanded by Gorman and minus the stray 34th New York Infantry, reached the far side of the woods and quickly opened fire on the remnants of *Jackson's* command to the west. The other two brigades, commanded by Brig. Gens. Napoleon J. T. Dana and Oliver O. Howard, lay down in the woods and awaited orders. As Gorman's men appeared at the western edge of the woods, troops from the commands of *Lawton* and *J. R. Jones* opened fire. Gorman later wrote, "Instantly my whole brigade became hotly engaged, giving and receiving the most deadly fire it has ever been my lot to witness."[39]

The Confederates rushed to meet the new Union threat in the West Woods. *Early's* brigade left its position to the west and moved into the West Woods. Earlier in the morning, *Pelham's* artillery had shifted south from Nicodemus Hill to a position on the heights west of the A. Poffenberger farm. *Lee* sent *Walker's* division from its reserve position south of Sharpsburg and the division of *McLaws* newly arrived from Harper's Ferry. Joining these divisions was the brigade of *Col. George T. Anderson* of *D. R. Jones'* division.

---

[39] Ibid., p. 311.

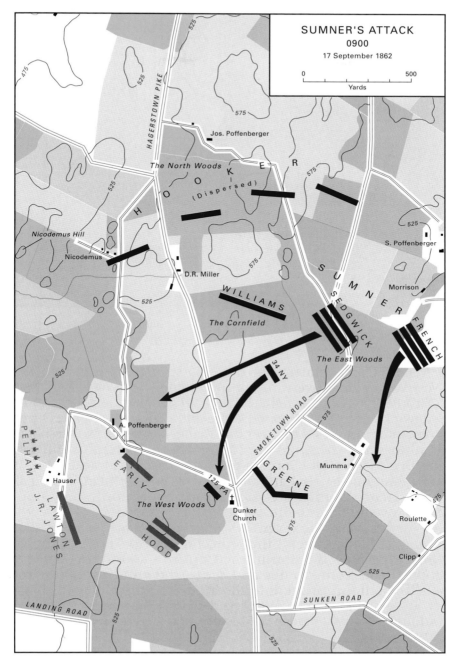

Jos. Poffenberger

The North Woods

HOOKER

(Dispersed)

HAGERSTOWN PIKE

575

575

Nicodemus Hill

525

Nicodemus

D.R. Miller

525

S. Poffenberger

Morrison

SUMNER

SEDGWICK

WILLIAMS

The Cornfield

The East Woods

FRENCH

34 NY

A. Poffenberger

SMOKETOWN ROAD

575

PELHAM

Hauser

EARLY

HOOD

The West Woods

125 PA

Dunker
Church

GREENE

Mumma

525

LAWTON

J.R. JONES

Roulette

Clipp

525

LANDING ROAD

525

SUNKEN ROAD

525

525

475

Map 8

Confederate Dead in Front of the Dunker Church

These Confederates, almost 8,000 strong, charged into the West Woods, first overrunning the isolated 34th New York and 125th Pennsylvania Infantries, then striking the left and rear of Sedgwick's division. (*Map 9*) Dana's and Howard's brigades leapt to their feet and tried to meet the attack, but it was too late. Like dominoes, they began to tumble northward with the Confederates in close pursuit. Gorman's brigade was also attacked, but it had more time to react and turned to meet the threat. Acting as a rear guard, Gorman's command withdrew northward, stopping now and then to fire a volley at its pursuers.

The remnants of Sedgwick's division fled across the Miller farm, where they sought the protection of Hooker's I Corps artillery. Williams' division in the Cornfield and Union artillery stopped the Confederates and drove them back to the West Woods. Sumner's attack into the West Woods had been a disaster. In less than thirty minutes, Sedgwick had been wounded and more than 40 percent of his division had been either killed or wounded.

As Sedgwick's division was collapsing, French's 5,700-man division, having split to the left of Sedgwick's advance into the West Woods and cheered on by the martial music of regimental bands, crossed the Mumma and Roulette farms and advanced

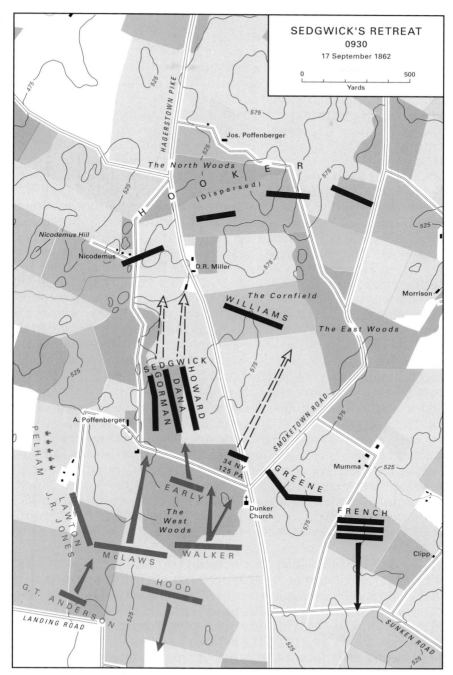

SEDGWICK'S RETREAT
0930
17 September 1862

0   500

Yards

Map 9

toward an old farm road, now known as the Sunken Road or Bloody Lane. (*Map 10*)

The Sunken Road joins Hagerstown Pike 500 yards south of Dunker Church, runs east about a thousand yards, and then turns south to Boonsboro Pike. Waiting in the road were almost 2,500 men of *D. H. Hill's* division. The left of *Hill's* line contained the brigade of *Brig. Gen. Robert E. Rodes*, which extended from near Hagerstown Pike to the lane leading to the William Roulette home. On *Rodes'* left, connecting with the pike, were remnants of the brigades of *Brig. Gen. Roswell S. Ripley, Col. D. K. McRae*, and *Col. A. H. Colquitt*, which had fought in the Cornfield earlier in the morning. On *Rodes'* right, the brigade of *Brig. Gen. George B. Anderson* continued the line another 200–300 yards. *Hill's* headquarters was about 300 yards south of the road, at the home of Henry Piper. As French's division approached, the Confederates strengthened their position by piling up fence rails while *Hill* sent urgent messages to *Lee* for more troops.

When French's men appeared on the high ground above the Sunken Road, the Confederates let loose a volley that staggered and halted the Union line. Both sides then settled down to pouring volley after volley into each other's ranks. Many officers on both sides soon found themselves on foot, their horses killed or wounded. *G. B. Anderson* received a wound in the foot that would lead to his death about one month after the battle. When a regimental commander stepped forward to replace *Anderson*, he was shot and killed. With casualties mounting on both sides, some of *Rodes'* men left the road several times and charged French's line; but the uncoordinated attacks were driven back.

Responding to *Hill's* pleas for assistance, *Lee* sent *Maj. Gen. Richard H. Anderson's* division, which had arrived from Harper's Ferry that morning. *Anderson's* men advanced rapidly through town and at roughly 1000 joined *Hill's* men in the Sunken Road. (*See Map 11.*) Shortly afterward, Richardson's division, which McClellan had ordered to march to the battlefield from guarding artillery east of the Antietam, arrived on the left of French's command.

Among the first of Richardson's units to reach the Sunken Road was Brig. Gen. Thomas F. Meagher's Irish Brigade, composed of immigrants recruited in New York City and Massachusetts. "On coming into close and fatal contact with the enemy," according to Meagher, "the officers and men of the brigade waved their swords and hats and gave three hearty cheers for their general, George McClellan, and the Army of the Potomac."[40] The Irishmen fired several volleys at the Confederates in the Sunken

---

[40] *OR*, p. 294.

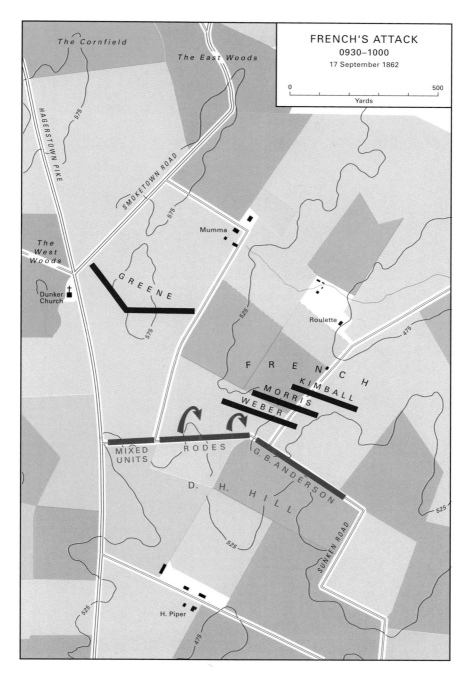

FRENCH'S ATTACK
0930–1000
17 September 1862

0   500
Yards

The Cornfield

The East Woods

HAGERSTOWN PIKE

SMOKETOWN ROAD

575

575

Mumma

The
West
Woods

Dunker
Church

GREENE

575

525

Roulette

475

F R E N C H

KIMBALL

MORRIS

WEBER

MIXED
UNITS

RODES

G. B. ANDERSON

D. H. HILL

525

525

SUNKEN ROAD

525

H. Piper

525

475

Map 10

Sunken Road, Looking Southeast, toward the Present-Day Stone Observation Tower

Sunken Road, Looking Northeast toward the Roulette Farm

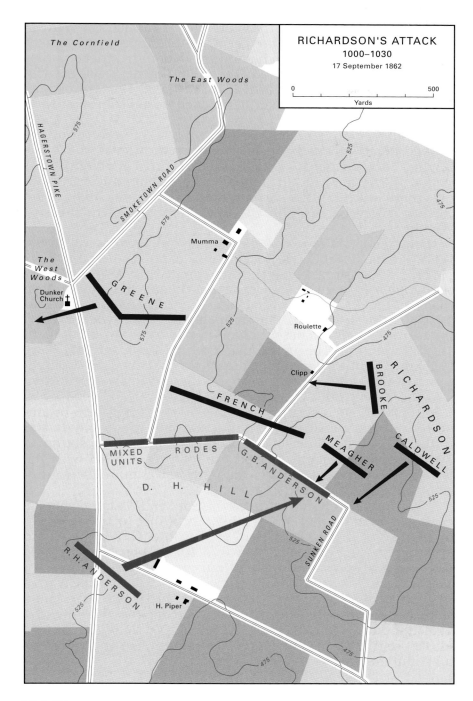

The Cornfield

The East Woods

RICHARDSON'S ATTACK
1000–1030
17 September 1862

0   500

Yards

HAGERSTOWN PIKE

SMOKETOWN ROAD

575

525

475

Mumma

The
West
Woods

Dunker
Church

GREENE

525

575

Roulette

475

Clipp

RICHARDSON

BROOKE

FRENCH

CALDWELL

MIXED
UNITS

RODES

MEAGHER

G. B. ANDERSON

D. H. HILL

525

SUNKEN ROAD

525

R. H. ANDERSON

525

H. Piper

475

475

Map 11

Road then charged up to the road and continued the fight at close range. Standing in the open, entire ranks of Meagher's men were shot down. Meagher, injured when his stricken horse fell on him, was carried from the field. Of the 1,400 men in Meagher's brigade when it arrived on the field, almost 1,000 lay dead or wounded. The remainder of Richardson's division soon arrived to join the fray.

While French's and Richardson's divisions fought along the Sunken Road, Greene's division charged into the West Woods, driving back elements of *Walker's* division. For roughly two hours Greene held his advanced position; but concerned that his command might be surrounded in the woods and not receiving requested support, the division fell back to the East Woods.

Upon Greene's retreat, *Walker's* men quickly reoccupied the West Woods. Greene's withdrawal also exposed the right flank of French's division, which the *3d Arkansas* and *27th North Carolina Infantries*, joined by groups from the mixed commands to the left of *Rodes'* brigade, attacked. (*Map 12*) French halted his attack on the Sunken Road and quickly faced westward to meet the threat. His command was soon joined by a portion of Richardson's division. The arrival near the East Woods of Maj. Gen. William F. Smith's division of the IV Corps caused the Confederates to withdraw. A portion of Smith's division pursued them into the West Woods but was driven back.

Around 1230, suffering from heavy casualties, lack of ammunition, and a misunderstanding of orders, the Confederates in the Sunken Road began to withdraw toward Sharpsburg. As Richardson's command crossed the road, now filled with the bodies of its former defenders, Richardson was mortally wounded by a fragment of shell.

The Confederate retreat from the Sunken Road uncovered a great gap in the center of *Lee's* line. According to *Longstreet*, after the loss of the Sunken Road, "The Confederate army would be cut in two and probably destroyed, for we were already badly whipped and were only holding our ground by sheer force of desperation."[41] Very few Confederates now stood in the way of a Union advance from the Sunken Road. Seeing two abandoned Confederate cannon south of the road, *Longstreet* had his staff man the guns while he led their horses. *D. H. Hill* grabbed a musket and, with roughly 200 Confederates, led an unsuccessful counterattack.

---

[41] James Longstreet, "The Invasion of Maryland," in *B&L*, p. 669.

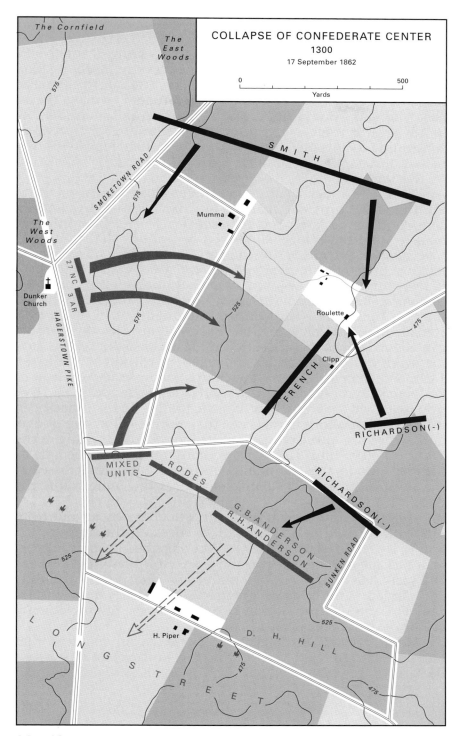

The Cornfield

The East Woods

COLLAPSE OF CONFEDERATE CENTER
1300
17 September 1862

0   500
Yards

SMOKETOWN ROAD

575

575

SMITH

Mumma

The West Woods

Dunker Church

27 NC   3 AR

HAGERSTOWN PIKE

575

525

Roulette

475

FRENCH

Clipp

RICHARDSON(-)

MIXED UNITS

RODES

G. B. ANDERSON
R. H. ANDERSON

RICHARDSON(-)

SUNKEN ROAD

525

525

H. Piper

D.   H.   HILL

475

475

L O N G S T R E E T

Map 12

With the Confederate center broken, one great Union push might have destroyed what was left of *Lee's* army. Franklin's IV Corps, Porter's V Corps, and the army's cavalry division stood poised for action. But McClellan made no attempt to capitalize on the Union success. "It would not be prudent to make the attack," he said, "our position on the right being ... considerably in advance of what it had been in the morning."[42] Instead of continuing to advance, McClellan ordered Richards' division to halt and to "hold that position against the enemy."[43] *Lee's* center was safe.

While the attack against the Sunken Road was in progress, Burnside's IX Corps, commanded by Cox, was attacking *Toombs'* command at the lower bridge. (*Map 13*) *Toombs* had only 400 men to hold the bridge, supported by another 100 from *Brig. Gen. Thomas F. Drayton's* brigade and a company of men from Jenkins' brigade, commanded by *Col. Joseph Walker*, both of *D. R. Jones'* division. The Union attack began about 1000, but the assaults were piecemeal, with only one or two regiments attacking at a time. The 11th Connecticut Infantry of Col. Edward Harland's brigade of Brig. Gen. Isaac P. Rodman's division began the assault; but after suffering heavy casualties, including the death of its commander, the regiment withdrew. While the 11th Connecticut Infantry attack was taking place, the rest of Rodman's division, along with a brigade of the Kanawha Division, searched for a ford south of the bridge. Rodman had been informed that a ford existed less than a mile below the bridge, but he discovered the crossing to be impracticable, being at the foot of a steep bluff rising more than 160 feet on the side of the creek. Rodman's command continued south and crossed at the waist-deep Snavely's Ford, two-thirds of a mile below the bridge.

After the withdrawal of the Connecticut troops, an aide from McClellan arrived near the bridge to check on the status of the attack. He reported to McClellan that there had been little progress. McClellan ordered Burnside "to assault the bridge at once and carry it at all hazards."[44] Around 1100 Burnside ordered the 2d Maryland and 6th New Hampshire Infantries of Brig. Gen. Samuel D. Sturgis' division to cross the bridge. *Toombs'* defenders, however, quickly drove them back.

Around noon McClellan's aide once again reported that Burnside's troops had yet to cross the bridge. McClellan sent the army's inspector general, Col. Delos B. Sackett, to order

[42] *OR*, p. 377.
[43] Ibid., p. 279.
[44] McClellan, *McClellan's Own Story*, p. 603.

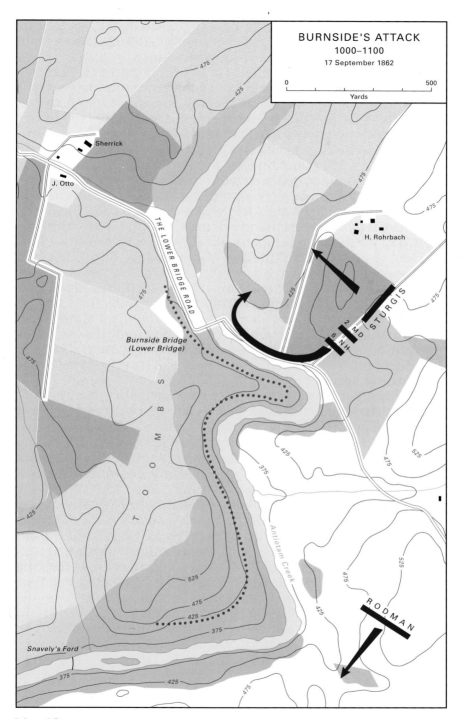

Map 13

Burnside, at the point of the bayonet if necessary, to capture the bridge immediately. McClellan instructed Sackett to remain with Burnside until the attack was successful.

Burnside next ordered the 51st New York and 51st Pennsylvania Infantries, also of Sturgis' division, to attempt to cross the bridge. Around 1300 the two regiments, supported by a howitzer positioned near the bridge abutment, charged across the bridge and reached the opposite bank. (*Map 14*) About the same time, Rodman's division made its crossing at Snavely's Ford. North of the bridge, several companies of the 28th Ohio Infantry of the Kanawha Division waded across the creek to the west bank. With the crossing of Burnside's troops at the bridge and other Union troops crossing above and below, *Toombs'* defense ended and the remnants of his command fell back toward Sharpsburg.

It had taken three hours for the IX Corps to secure a crossing, and it would be another two hours before Burnside could get the entire corps across the creek. McClellan was unhappy with the delay and ordered Burnside to continue his attack. Around 1500 the IX Corps began climbing the slopes toward Sharpsburg. As the troops approached the town, a Union signal detachment east of Antietam Creek signaled to Burnside, "Look out well on your left; the enemy are moving a strong force in that direction."[45] It is unknown whether Burnside actually saw the warning message.

The approaching Confederates were elements of *A. P. Hill's* division arriving from Harper's Ferry. *Hill* had left the brigade of *Brig. Gen. Edward L. Thomas* at Harper's Ferry to continue removing captured supplies, but he himself headed toward Sharpsburg with his five remaining brigades. Around 1430, after a seventeen-mile forced march, the head of *Hill's* command reached Sharpsburg; *Lee* quickly ordered it toward Burnside's advancing columns. (*See Map 15.*) While the brigades of *Col. J. M. Brockenbrough* and *Brig. Gen. William D. Pender* guarded *Hill's* right, the brigades of *Brig. Gens. L. O'B. Branch, Maxcy Gregg,* and *J. J. Archer* charged into Burnside's left. The strenuous march had seriously depleted their strength, however, and the three attacking Confederate brigades numbered fewer than 2,000 men.[46] In fact, *Archer's* brigade alone numbered only 350 men.[47]

While Brig. Gen. Orlando B. Willcox's division, on the right of Burnside's attack, continued its advance to the outskirts of Sharpsburg, the sudden attack on the Union left halted Rodman's division. A portion of the Kanawha Division was ordered

---

[45] *OR*, p. 138.
[46] Ibid., p. 981.
[47] Ibid., p. 1000.

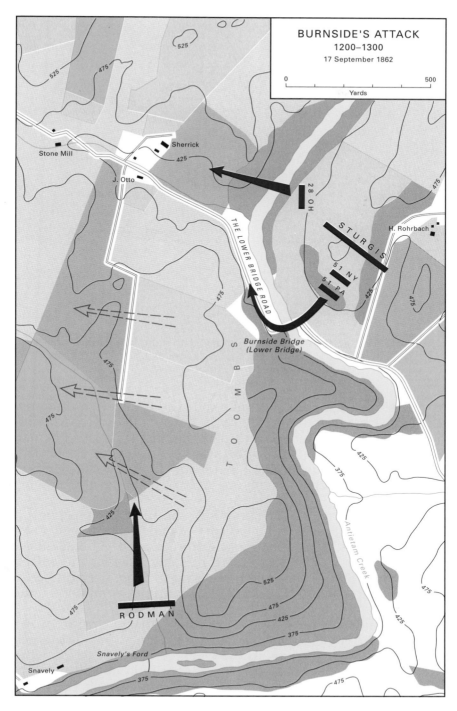

BURNSIDE'S ATTACK
1200–1300
17 September 1862

0   500
Yards

Stone Mill

Sherrick

J. Otto

425

28 OH

STURGIS

H. Rohrbach

THE LOWER BRIDGE ROAD

51 NY

51 PA

Burnside Bridge
(Lower Bridge)

T O O M B S

Antietam Creek

RODMAN

Snavely's Ford

Snavely

Map 14

The Charge across the Burnside Bridge, Antietam, *Edwin Forbes. The drawing shows the charge of the 51st New York and 51st Pennsylvania Infantries across Burnside Bridge.*

up the slope to support Rodman, but the troops had difficulty distinguishing friend from foe in the battle smoke. Troop identification was made even more difficult because some of *Hill*'s men were wearing portions of Union uniforms captured at Harper's Ferry. In the confusion the portion of the Kanawha Division ordered to support Rodman was outflanked by *Gregg* and fell back.

For the IX Corps' effort to climb the hill to Sharpsburg, it suffered 2,000 casualties, including General Rodman, killed early in the attack. Rodman was the third Union general officer to be killed or mortally wounded this day. Toward the end of the fighting, *Branch* was killed, bringing to three the number of Confederate general officers killed or mortally wounded in the battle.

It was now around 1700 and growing dark. Unsure of the size of the Confederate force attacking his left, Burnside ordered the IX Corps to withdraw to the creek. As the sun set on what would become known as the bloodiest single day of the war, the IX Corps established a defensive perimeter near the lower bridge. *Lee*'s exhausted troops on the heights above the bridge were content to remain in place.

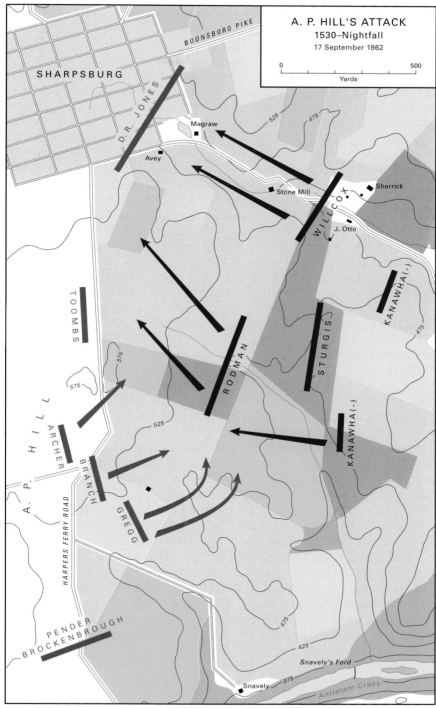

A. P. HILL'S ATTACK
1530–Nightfall
17 September 1862

0   500
Yards

SHARPSBURG

BOONSBORO PIKE

D. R. JONES

Magraw

Avey

Stone Mill

Sherrick

WILLCOX

J. Otto

KANAWHA(−)

TOOMBS

STURGIS

575

RODMAN

575

525

KANAWHA(−)

A. P. HILL

ARCHER

BRANCH

HARPERS FERRY ROAD

GREGG

525

475

PENDER

BROCKENBROUGH

425

Snavely's Ford

Snavely — 375

Antietam Creek

Map 15

The following morning, 18 September, the two armies remained in position. McClellan wrote, "To renew the attack again on the 18th or defer it, with the chance of the enemy's retirement after a day of suspense, were the questions before me."[48] McClellan decided to wait and issued orders to renew the attack on 19 September. *Lee*, however, was ready to keep up the fight. An additional 5,000–6,000 stragglers had caught up with the army; according to one of *Lee*'s officers, the Confederate commander hoped to turn McClellan's flank near the bend of the Potomac River west of Nicodemus Hill. Due to the large amount of Union artillery in the area, the plan was abandoned.[49] Unable to outflank McClellan on the Maryland side of the river, *Lee* withdrew his army to Virginia during the night of 18 September, hoping to recross the Potomac at Williamsport and attack McClellan's rear. The plan, however, was thwarted by the poor physical condition of his army; *Lee* decided to remain in Virginia.[50]

On the morning of 19 September McClellan discovered that the Confederates had withdrawn. A feeble Union pursuit resulted in a sharp fight at Boteler's Ford the following day, but McClellan was content to remain in Maryland and claim victory. *Lee*'s army withdrew into the Shenandoah Valley to continue to gather supplies.

Weeks passed. In early October Lincoln visited the Union army near Sharpsburg to urge McClellan to cross into Virginia and give battle. McClellan, however, insisted that he needed more men and supplies before beginning another campaign. On 6 October Lincoln telegraphed McClellan to "cross the Potomac and give battle to the enemy or drive him south."[51]

On 10 October, while the Army of the Potomac remained in the Sharpsburg area, 1,800 men of *Stuart*'s cavalry crossed the Potomac near Williamsport and reentered Maryland on an armed reconnaissance. The troops rode to Chambersburg, Pennsylvania, then eastward, gathering intelligence and much-needed horses while pursued by McClellan's cavalry. After circling around McClellan's encamped army, *Stuart*'s men recrossed the Potomac near Leesburg on 12 October.

McClellan was still at Sharpsburg on 25 October, when he wired to Washington that he remained unable to move because his horses were suffering from sore-tongue and fatigue. An exasperated Lincoln responded: "I have just read your dispatch

---

[48] Ibid., p. 32.
[49] Harsh, *Sounding the Shallows*, pp. 214–15.
[50] *OR*, pt. 2, p. 626.
[51] Ibid., p. 72.

about sore-tongued and fatigued horses. Will you pardon me for asking what the horses of your army have done since the battle of Antietam that fatigues anything?"[52]

The Army of the Potomac finally began to cross the Potomac River on 26 October but did not complete the crossing for almost a week. Lincoln finally reached the end of his patience and on 7 November relieved McClellan of command and replaced him with Ambrose Burnside.

Summary

For the North, the fight along Antietam Creek became known as the Battle of Antietam. In the South, it became known as the Battle of Sharpsburg. Of the nearly 70,000 Federal troops actually engaged in the battle, nearly 13,000 were killed, wounded, or missing; the approximately 35,000 Confederates engaged lost almost as many.

Writing to his wife, McClellan said, "Those in whose judgment I rely tell me that I fought the battle splendidly and that is was a masterpiece of art."[53] In truth, however, McClellan missed a series of opportunities. By failing to commit his forces to battle on 15 and 16 September, McClellan squandered a chance to exploit his numerical superiority. On 17 September McClellan's piecemeal commitment of only a portion of his command during the battle—"in driblets," as General Sumner later described it[54]—failed to deliver a knockout blow to destroy the *Army of Northern Virginia*. McClellan's decision not to renew the battle on 18 September, with the same if not greater opportunity of success as the previous day, as well as his failure to energetically pursue the Confederate army on 19 September, allowed *Lee* to withdraw to the safety of the Virginia shore.

Lee, like McClellan, generally believed that the role of an army commander was to bring his army to the battlefield and allow his subordinates to handle the tactical details.[55] But the desperate situation on 17 September forced *Lee* to become actively involved in the battle, despite injuries to both his hands. He spent most of the day on the heights in the area of the present-day National Cemetery, where he watched the progress of the

---

[52] Ibid., p. 485.

[53] Sears, *Papers of George B. McClellan*, p. 469.

[54] *Report on the Conduct of the War*, 8 vols. (Wilmington: Broadfoot Publishing Co., 1998), 1: 368.

[55] Douglas Southall Freeman, *R. E. Lee: A Biography*, 4 vols. (New York: Charles Scribner's Sons, 1935), 4: 168–69.

battle and personally dispatched various units to endangered portions of the field. He sent the commands of *Walker, McLaws,* and *G. T. Anderson* just in time to halt Sedgwick's advance on the Confederate left flank; rushed *R. H. Anderson* to support *D. H. Hill's* defense of the Confederate center; and, when *A. P. Hill's* division began arriving at Sharpsburg in the afternoon, hurried *Hill's* command to save the Confederate right flank.

Although the Confederates had been forced out of Maryland, *Lee's* campaign had been a partial success. *Jackson's* capture of Harper's Ferry provided the Confederates with a large amount of supplies, including clothing, shoes, thousands of small arms and ammunition, and over seventy pieces of artillery. In addition, another major Federal offensive in Virginia had been delayed, albeit only briefly. In mid-December Burnside, now commanding The Army of the Potomac, attempted to interpose his command between *Lee* and Richmond. The maneuver culminated in a Union defeat at the Battle of Fredericksburg.

Although Antietam was not the decisive Union victory for which Lincoln had hoped, it did give the president an opportunity to strike at the Confederacy politically, psychologically, and economically. On 22 September Lincoln issued the preliminary Emancipation Proclamation, declaring that the Federal government would after 1 January 1863 consider slaves in any state in rebellion against the Federal government to be free. The proclamation had no immediate effect behind Confederate lines, nor did it free any slaves in states still in the Union. Nevertheless, Lincoln's proclamation would be the Federal government's first official step toward the abolition of human slavery.

Shortly after the battle, McClellan wrote that Confederate dreams of invading Pennsylvania had dissipated forever.[56] During the coming months, however, *Lee* would wait for another opportunity to cross his army north of the Potomac. The summer of 1863 would find the *Army of Northern Virginia* and the Army of the Potomac, the latter commanded by the recently promoted Maj. Gen. George Meade, confronting each other at the small Pennsylvania town of Gettysburg.

---

[56] Sears, *Papers of George B. McClellan,* p. 473.

FURTHER READINGS

Bradford, Ned, ed. *Battles and Leaders of the Civil War*. New York: Grammercy Books, 2001.

Harsh, Joseph L. *Confederate Tide Rising: Robert E. Lee and the Making of Southern Strategy*. Kent, Ohio: Kent State University Press, 1998.

————. *Sounding the Shallows: A Confederate Companion for the Maryland Campaign of 1862*. Kent, Ohio: Kent State University Press, 2000.

————. *Taken at the Flood: Lee and Confederate Strategy in the Maryland Campaign*. Kent, Ohio: Kent State University Press, 1999.

Murfin, James V. *The Gleam of Bayonets: The Battle of Antietam and Robert E. Lee's Maryland Campaign, 1862*. Baton Rouge: Louisiana State University Press, 2004.

Sears, Stephen W. *Landscape Turned Red: The Battle of Antietam*. Norwalk, Conn.: Easton Press, 1988.

U.S. War Department. *The War of the Rebellion: A Compilation of the Official Records of the Union and Confederate Armies*, 70 vols. Washington, D.C.: Government Printing Office, 1893, ser. 1, vol. 19, pts. 1 and 2.

CHRONOLOGY

Times are approximate and based on those given in the after-action reports by unit commanders or in postwar reminiscences.

4–7 September 1862

The *Army of Northern Virginia*, commanded by *General Robert E. Lee*, crosses the Potomac River near *Lees*burg and marches to Frederick, Maryland.

The Army of the Potomac, commanded by Maj. Gen. George B. McClellan, leaves Washington in pursuit of *Lee*.

9 September

Lee issues Special Orders 191, detailing his plan to capture Union garrisons at Martinsburg and Harper's Ferry.

10 September

Lee and *Maj. Gen. James Longstreet* march to Hagerstown. *Maj. Gen. D. H. Hill's* division halts at Boonsboro as rear guard.

Maj. Gen. Thomas J. Jackson marches to capture the Union garrison at Martinsburg.

The divisions of *Maj. Gens. Lafayette McLaws* and *Richard H. Anderson* approach Harper's Ferry from the east.

Brig. Gen. John G. Walker's division crosses the Potomac River into Virginia and approaches Harper's Ferry from the south.

12 September

The Army of the Potomac begins arriving at Frederick.

Jackson reaches Martinsburg, but the Union garrison flees to Harper's Ferry.

13 September

McClellan arrives at Frederick.

A soldier in McClellan's army finds a copy of *Lee's* Special Orders 191. The document is given to McClellan, who plans to attack the Confederates the following day at South Mountain.

Jackson marches from Martinsburg to Harper's Ferry.

In the evening *Lee* receives information from *Maj. Gen. James E. B. Stuart* that McClellan's army has arrived at Frederick.

To delay an expected Union advance, *Lee* orders *D. H. Hill* to defend Turner's and Fox's Gaps on South Mountain. *Longstreet* is sent to support *Hill*. *McLaws* sends a portion of his command to defend Crampton's Gap.

14 September

The siege of Harper's Ferry begins.

The Battle of South Mountain occurs. Union forces take Crampton's Gap.

During the night *Lee* decides to withdraw his outnumbered forces from Turner's and Fox's Gaps and falls back to Sharpsburg.

15 September

Lee, along with *Longstreet*, the divisions of *Brig. Gen. D. R. Jones* and *D. H. Hill*, and part of *Stuart's* cavalry, arrives at Sharpsburg.

Harper's Ferry surrenders. *Lee* orders the Confederate troops there to march to Sharpsburg as soon as possible. *Maj. Gen. Ambrose P. Hill's* division remains at Harper's Ferry to parole prisoners and gather supplies.

The Army of the Potomac arrives near Sharpsburg. McClellan replaces Maj. Gen. Ambrose E. Burnside with Maj. Gen. Joseph Hooker in command of the army's right wing and puts Burnside in command of the left wing.

16 September

0730: *Jackson*'s command reaches Sharpsburg, reuniting with *D. H. Hill's* division.

Walker's division arrives at Sharpsburg.

1530–1600: Hooker's I Corps crosses Antietam Creek north of Sharpsburg to turn *Lee's* left flank. A portion of Brig. Gen. George G. Meade's division, leading Hooker's corps, skirmishes with *Brig. Gen. John B. Hood*'s division near the East Woods.

In response to Hooker's request for reinforcements, McClellan orders Maj. Gen. Edwin V. Sumner's XII Corps, commanded by Maj. Gen. Joseph K. F. Mansfield, from the center to the right wing.

Lee sends *Jackson*, with his divisions commanded by *Brig. Gens. John R. Jones* and *A. R. Lawton*, to support *Hood*. *Walker*'s division remains in reserve south of the town.

1930: McClellan, after learning that Harper's Ferry has surrendered, orders Maj. Gen. William B. Franklin's VI Corps to join the army at Sharpsburg.

2400: Mansfield's XII Corps crosses Antietam Creek to join Hooker's I Corps.

17 September

0600: *McLaws'* and *R. H. Anderson*'s divisions arrive at Sharpsburg.

Hooker's I Corps begins its attack south on Hagerstown Pike and Smoketown Road, initially meeting with great success at the Cornfield.

0700: Called to assist by *Jackson*, whose lines are collapsing, *Hood*'s division launches a counterattack from the West Woods against Hooker's I Corps in the Cornfield.

0730: Acting on orders received the night before, *A. P. Hill*'s division begins a forced march from Harper's Ferry to Sharpsburg.

Mansfield's XII Corps arrives in the East Woods. Brig. Gen. Alpheus S. Williams' division of the XII Corps drives *Hood*'s division from the Cornfield back into the West Woods. Mansfield is mortally wounded, and Williams assumes command of the division.

0800: Maj. Gen. John Sedgwick's and Brig. Gen. William H. French's divisions of Sumner's II Corps cross Antietam Creek to support Hooker's I Corps. Sumner leaves behind his third division, command by Maj. Gen. Israel B. Richardson, to guard artillery.

0900: Sedgwick's division attacks into the West Woods. French's division attacks at the Sunken Road against the division of *D. H. Hill*. *Hill* sends an urgent request to *Lee* for reinforcement.

One of Sedgwick's regiments, the 34th New York Infantry, becomes separated from the rest of the division and halts near Dunker Church, where it finds the 125th Pennsylvania Infantry of Williams' division, which had ended up there some time earlier.

Brig. Gen. Isaac P. Rodman's division of Burnside's IX Corps is sent to outflank the lower bridge by crossing Antietam Creek at Snavely's Ford.

Brig. Gen. George S. Greene's division of the XII Corps reaches the plateau east of the West Woods.

Hooker is slightly wounded, and Meade assumes command of the I Corps.

0930: Sedgwick's division is driven out of the West Woods by the division of *Walker*, sent from its reserve position south of Sharpsburg; the division of *McLaws*, newly arrived from Harper's Ferry; the brigade of *Brig. Gen Jubal A. Early*, from its station west of the West Woods; and the brigade of *Col. G. T. Anderson* of *D. R. Jones'* division. The Confederate advance into the Cornfield is stopped by Union artillery and Williams' division, which had remained in the Cornfield.

1000: *D. H. Hill's* division, defending the Sunken Road against French's attack, is reinforced by the division of *R. H. Anderson*, which had just arrived from Harper's Ferry.

Spearheaded by the 11th Connecticut Infantry, the IX Corps attack on *Brig. Gen. Robert Toombs'* brigade at the lower bridge begins.

51

1030: After crossing Antietam Creek, Richardson's division of the II Corps joins French's attack on the Sunken Road.

Greene's division occupies the West Woods.

1100: The 2d Maryland and 6th New Hampshire Infantries of the IX Corps unsuccessfully attempt to cross the lower bridge.

Greene's division withdraws from the West Woods and falls back to the East Woods. *Walker's* division reoccupies the West Woods.

The *27th North Carolina* and *3d Arkansas Infantries*, along with portions of other Confederate commands, attack the right flank of French's division. Maj. Gen. William F. Smith's division of the VI Corps drives the Confederates into the West Woods.

1230: *D. H. Hill's* Confederates withdraw from the Sunken Road. Richardson's division pursues them, but McClellan orders it to halt its advance, inadvertently saving *Lee's* center.

1300: The 51st New York and 51st Pennsylvania Infantries of the IX Corps cross the lower bridge. The remainder of the IX Corps begins to cross the bridge.

South of the lower bridge, Rodman's division crosses Antietam Creek at Snavely's Ford.

North of the lower bridge, elements of the 28th Ohio Infantry cross Antietam Creek.

With Union troops above, below, and across from him, *Toombs* withdraws to Sharpsburg.

1430: *A. P. Hill's* division begins arriving near Sharpsburg.

1500: Having finished crossing Antietam Creek, the IX Corps advances on Sharpsburg.

1600: *A. P. Hill's* division attacks the left flank of the IX Corps and successfully halts the Union advance toward the town.

1700: The IX Corps falls back to the lower bridge.

18 September

McClellan decides not to attack this day but instead issues orders to attack on 19 September.

Lee wishes to renew the fight, but he calculates that the odds are too much against him and withdraws his army back into Virginia during the night.

19 September

In the morning McClellan learns that the Confederates withdrew during the night. He chooses not to pursue them.

ORDER OF BATTLE, 17 SEPTEMBER 1862[1]

Army of the Potomac, United States Army
Maj. Gen. George B. McClellan

I Corps (Maj. Gen. Joseph Hooker)
    1st Division (Brig. Gen. Abner Doubleday)
        1st Brigade (Col. Walter J. Phelps, Jr.)
            22d New York Infantry
            24th New York Infantry
            30th New York Infantry
            84th New York Infantry (14th Militia)
            2d U.S. Sharpshooters

        2d Brigade (Col. William P. Wainwright)
            7th Indiana Infantry
            56th New York Infantry
            76th New York Infantry
            95th New York Infantry

        3d Brigade (Brig. Gen. Marsena R. Patrick)
            21st New York Infantry
            23d New York Infantry
            35th New York Infantry
            80th New York Infantry (20th Militia)

        4th Brigade (Brig. Gen. John Gibbon)
            19th Indiana Infantry
            2d Wisconsin Infantry
            6th Wisconsin Infantry
            7th Wisconsin Infantry

        Artillery (Capt. J. Albert Monroe)
            New Hampshire Light, 1st Battery
            1st New York Light, Battery L
            1st Rhode Island Light, Battery D
            4th U.S. Artillery, Battery B

---

[1] U.S. War Department, *The War of the Rebellion: A Compilation of the Official Records of the Union and Confederate Armies*, 70 vols. (Washington, D.C.: Government Printing Office, 1893), ser. 1, vol. 19, pt. 1 (hereafter cited as *OR*), pp. 169–80, 803–10.

2d Division (Brig. Gen. James B. Ricketts)
    1st Brigade (Brig. Gen. Abram Duryea)
        97th New York Infantry
        104th New York Infantry
        105th New York Infantry
        107th New York Infantry

    2d Brigade (Col. William A. Christian)
        26th New York Infantry
        94th New York Infantry
        88th Pennsylvania Infantry
        90th Pennsylvania Infantry

    3d Brigade (Brig. Gen. George L. Hartsuff)
        16th Maine Infantry (on detached duty)
        12th Massachusetts Infantry
        13th Massachusetts Infantry
        83d New York Infantry (9th Militia)
        11th Pennsylvania Infantry

    Artillery
        1st Pennsylvania Light, Battery F
        Pennsylvania Light, Battery C

3d Division (Brig. Gen. George G. Meade)
    1st Brigade (Brig. Gen. Truman Seymour)
        1st Pennsylvania Infantry
        2d Pennsylvania Infantry
        5th Pennsylvania Infantry
        6th Pennsylvania Infantry
        13th Pennsylvania Infantry

    2d Brigade (Col. Albert L. Magilton)
        3d Pennsylvania Infantry
        4th Pennsylvania Infantry
        7th Pennsylvania Infantry
        8th Pennsylvania Infantry

    3d Brigade (Col. Thomas F. Gallagher)
        9th Pennsylvania Reserves
        10th Pennsylvania Reserves
        11th Pennsylvania Reserves
        12th Pennsylvania Reserves

Artillery
     1st Pennsylvania Light, Batteries A and B
     1st Pennsylvania Light, Battery G
     (on detached duty)
     5th U.S. Artillery, Battery C

II Corps (Maj. Gen. Edwin V. Sumner)
    1st Division (Maj. Gen. Israel B. Richardson)

      1st Brigade (Brig. Gen. John C. Caldwell)
        5th New Hampshire Infantry
        7th New York Infantry
        61st New York Infantry
        64th New York Infantry
        81st Pennsylvania Infantry

      2d Brigade (Brig. Gen. Thomas F. Meagher)
        29th Massachusetts Infantry
        63d New York Infantry
        69th New York Infantry
        88th New York Infantry

      3d Brigade (Col. John R. Brooke)
        2d Delaware Infantry
        52d New York Infantry
        57th New York Infantry
        66th New York Infantry
        53d Pennsylvania Infantry

      Artillery
        1st New York Light, Battery B
        4th U.S. Artillery, Batteries A and C

    2d Division (Maj. Gen. John Sedgwick)
      1st Brigade (Brig. Gen. Willis A. Gorman)
        15th Massachusetts Infantry
        1st Minnesota Infantry
        34th New York Infantry (2d Militia)
        82d New York Infantry
        Massachusetts Sharpshooters, 1st
          Company
        Minnesota Sharpshooters, 2d Company

      2d Brigade (Brig. Gen. Oliver O. Howard)
        69th Pennsylvania Infantry
        71st Pennsylvania Infantry

72d Pennsylvania Infantry
106th Pennsylvania Infantry

3d Brigade (Brig. Gen. Napoleon J. T. Dana)
19th Massachusetts Infantry
20th Massachusetts Infantry
7th Michigan Infantry
42d New York Infantry
59th New York Infantry

Artillery
1st Rhode Island Light, Battery A
1st U.S. Artillery, Battery I

3d Division (Brig. Gen. William H. French)
1st Brigade (Brig. Gen. Nathan Kimball)
14th Indiana Infantry
8th Ohio Infantry
132d Pennsylvania Infantry
7th West Virginia Infantry

2d Brigade (Col. Dwight Morris)
14th Connecticut Infantry
108th New York Infantry
130th Pennsylvania Infantry

3d Brigade (Brig. Gen. Max Weber)
1st Delaware Infantry
5th Maryland Infantry
4th New York Infantry

Unassigned Artillery
1st New York Light, Battery G
1st Rhode Island Light, Batteries B and G

V Corps (Maj. Gen. Fitz John Porter)
1st Division (Maj. Gen. George W. Morell)
1st Brigade (Col. James Barnes)
2d Maine Infantry
18th Massachusetts Infantry
22d Massachusetts Infantry
1st Michigan Infantry
13th New York Infantry
25th New York Infantry
118th Pennsylvania Infantry
Massachusetts Sharpshooters, 2d Company

2d Brigade (Brig. Gen. Charles Griffin)
    2d District of Columbia Infantry
    9th Massachusetts Infantry
    32d Massachusetts Infantry
    4th Michigan Infantry
    14th New York Infantry
    62d Pennsylvania Infantry

3d Brigade (Col. T. B. W. Stockton)
    20th Maine Infantry
    16th Michigan Infantry
    12th New York Infantry
    17th New York Infantry
    44th New York Infantry
    83d Pennsylvania Infantry
    Michigan Sharpshooters, Brady's Company

Artillery
    Massachusetts Light, Battery C
    1st Rhode Island Light, Battery C
    5th U.S. Artillery, Battery D

Undersigned
    1st U.S. Sharpshooters

2d Division (Brig. Gen. George Sykes)
    1st Brigade (Lt. Col. Robert C. Buchanan)
        3d U.S. Infantry
        4th U.S. Infantry
        12th U.S. Infantry (2 battalions)
        14th U.S. Infantry (2 battalions)

2d Brigade (Maj. Charles S. Lovell)
    1st U.S. Infantry
    2d U.S. Infantry
    6th U.S. Infantry
    10th U.S. Infantry
    11th U.S. Infantry
    17th U.S. Infantry

3d Brigade (Col. Gouverneur K. Warren)
    5th New York Infantry
    10th New York Infantry

Artillery
    1st U.S. Artillery, Batteries E and G
    5th U.S. Artillery, Batteries I and K

3d Division (Brig. Gen. Andrew A. Humphreys)[2]
    1st Brigade (Brig. Gen. Erastus B. Tyler)
        91st Pennsylvania Infantry
        126th Pennsylvania Infantry
        129th Pennsylvania Infantry
        134th Pennsylvania Infantry

    2d Brigade (Col. Peter H. Allabach)
        123d Pennsylvania Infantry
        131st Pennsylvania Infantry
        133d Pennsylvania Infantry
        155th Pennsylvania Infantry

    Artillery (Capt. Lucius N. Robinson)
        1st New York Light, Battery C
        1st Ohio Light, Battery L

Artillery Reserve (Lt. Col. William Hays)
    1st Battalion, New York Light, Batteries A,
        B, C, and D
    New York Light, 5th Battery
    1st U.S. Artillery, Battery K
    4th U.S. Artillery, Battery G

VI Corps (Maj. Gen. William B. Franklin)
    1st Division (Maj. Gen. Henry W. Slocum)
        1st Brigade (Col. Alfred T. A. Torbert)
            1st New Jersey Infantry
            2d New Jersey Infantry
            3d New Jersey Infantry
            4th New Jersey Infantry

        2d Brigade (Col. Joseph J. Bartlett)
            5th Maine Infantry
            16th New York Infantry
            27th Pennsylvania Infantry
            96th Pennsylvania Infantry

        3d Brigade (Brig. Gen. John Newton)
            18th New York Infantry

---

[2] This division did not arrive on the battlefield until early on the morning of 18 September.

31st New York Infantry
32d New York Infantry
95th New York Infantry

Artillery (Capt. Emory Upton)
    Maryland Light, Battery A
    Massachusetts Light, Battery A
    New Jersey Light, Battery A
    2d U.S. Artillery, Battery D

2d Division (Maj. Gen. William F. Smith)
    1st Brigade (Brig. Gen. Winfield S. Hancock)
        6th Maine Infantry
        43d New York Infantry
        49th New York Infantry·
        137th Pennsylvania Infantry
        5th Wisconsin Infantry

    2d Brigade (Brig. Gen. W. T. H. Brooks)
        2d Vermont Infantry
        3d Vermont Infantry
        4th Vermont Infantry
        5th Vermont Infantry
        6th Vermont Infantry

    3d Brigade (Col. William H. Irwin)
        7th Maine Infantry
        20th New York Infantry
        33d New York Infantry
        49th New York Infantry
        77th New York Infantry

    Artillery (Capt. Romeyn B. Ayres)
        Maryland Light, Battery B
        New York Light, 1st Battery
        5th U.S. Artillery, Battery F

Couch's Division (Maj. Gen. Darius N. Couch)[3]
    1st Brigade (Brig. Gen. Charles Devens, Jr.)
        7th Massachusetts Infantry

---

[3] This division was previously part of the IV Corps. That corps was disbanded in August 1862, and its divisions were separated and assigned to various commands. The 1st Division (Couch) was assigned to support the IV Corps during the Maryland Campaign. It did not arrive on the Antietam battlefield until early in the morning on 18 September.

10th Massachusetts Infantry
36th Massachusetts Infantry
2d Rhode Island Infantry

2d Brigade (Brig. Gen. Albion P. Howe)
62d New York Infantry
93d Pennsylvania Infantry
98th Pennsylvania Infantry
102d Pennsylvania Infantry
139th Pennsylvania Infantry

3d Brigade (Brig. Gen. John Cochrane)
65th New York Infantry
67th New York Infantry
122d New York Infantry
23d Pennsylvania Infantry
61st Pennsylvania Infantry
82d Pennsylvania Infantry

Artillery
New York Light, 3d Battery
1st Pennsylvania Light, Batteries C and D
2d U.S. Artillery, Battery G

IX Corps (Brig. Gen. Jacob D. Cox)[4]
1st Division (Brig. Gen. Orlando B. Willcox)
1st Brigade (Col. Benjamin C. Christ)
28th Massachusetts Infantry
17th Michigan Infantry
79th New York Infantry
50th Pennsylvania Infantry

---

[4] In mid-September 1862 Maj. Gen. Ambrose E. Burnside, commanding the IX Corps, was assigned command of the right wing of the Army of the Potomac, composed of the IX and I Corps. The IX Corps was temporarily placed under the command of Maj. Gen. Jesse L. Reno. After Reno was killed on 14 September, Brig. Gen. Jacob D. Cox assumed temporary command of the corps. The following day, 15 September, the organization of the right wing of the army was suspended; the I Corps commander, General Hooker, was ordered to report directly to General McClellan. General Burnside was assigned command of the left of the army, which consisted only of the IX Corps. Orders from general headquarters were forwarded through Burnside to General Cox. *OR*, pp. 290, 297.

2d Brigade (Col. Thomas Welch)
8th Michigan Infantry
46th New York Infantry
45th Pennsylvania Infantry
100th Pennsylvania Infantry

Artillery
Massachusetts Light, 8th Battery
2d U.S. Artillery, Battery E

2d Division (Brig. Gen. Samuel D. Sturgis)
1st Brigade (Brig. Gen. James Nagle)
2d Maryland Infantry
6th New Hampshire Infantry
9th New Hampshire Infantry
48th Pennsylvania Infantry

2d Brigade (Brig. Gen. Edward Ferrero)
21st Massachusetts Infantry
35th Massachusetts Infantry
51st New York Infantry
51st Pennsylvania Infantry

Artillery
Pennsylvania Light, Battery D
4th U.S. Artillery, Battery E

3d Division (Brig. Gen. Isaac P. Rodman)
1st Brigade (Col. Harrison S. Fairchild)
9th New York Infantry
89th New York Infantry
103d New York Infantry

2d Brigade (Col. Edward Harland)
8th Connecticut Infantry
11th Connecticut Infantry
16th Connecticut Infantry
4th Rhode Island Infantry

Artillery
5th U.S. Artillery, Battery A

Kanawha Division (Col. Eliakim P. Scammon)
1st Brigade (Col. Hugh Ewing)
12th Ohio Infantry

23d Ohio Infantry
30th Ohio Infantry
Ohio Light Artillery, 1st Battery
Gilmore's Company, West Virginia Cavalry
Harrison's Company, West Virginia Cavalry

2d Brigade (Col. George Crook)
11th Ohio Infantry
28th Ohio Infantry
36th Ohio Infantry
Schambeck's Company, Chicago Dragoons
Kentucky Light Artillery, Simmond's Battery

Unassigned
6th New York Cavalry (8 companies)
Ohio Cavalry, 3d Independent Company
3d U.S. Artillery, Batteries L and M

XII Corps (Maj. Gen. Joseph K. F. Mansfield)

1st Division (Brig. Gen. Alpheus S. Williams)[5]
1st Brigade (Brig. Gen Samuel W. Crawford)
5th Connecticut Infantry (on detached duty)
10th Maine Infantry
28th New York Infantry
46th Pennsylvania Infantry
124th Pennsylvania Infantry
125th Pennsylvania Infantry
128th Pennsylvania Infantry

3d Brigade (Brig. Gen. George H. Gordon)
27th Indiana Infantry
2d Massachusetts Infantry
13th New Jersey Infantry
107th New York Infantry
3d Wisconsin Infantry
Zouaves d'Afrique (Pennsylvania)[6]

2d Division (Brig. Gen. George S. Greene)
1st Brigade (Lt. Col. Hector Tyndale)
5th Ohio Infantry

_____

[5] Prior to the Battle of Antietam, the organization of the 2d Brigade was ended and all regiments of the brigade were transferred to the 1st and 3d Brigades.
[6] No officers being present, the enlisted men were attached to the 2d Massachusetts Infantry.

7th Ohio Infantry
29th Ohio Infantry
66th Ohio Infantry
28th Pennsylvania Infantry

2d Brigade (Col. Henry J. Stainrook)
3d Maryland Infantry
102d New York Infantry
109th Pennsylvania Infantry
(on detached duty)
111th Pennsylvania Infantry

3d Brigade (Col. William B. Goodrich)
3d Delaware Infantry
Purnell Legion (Maryland)
60th New York Infantry
78th New York Infantry

Artillery (Capt. Clermont L. Best)
Maine Light, 4th Battery
Maine Light, 6th Battery
1st New York Light, Battery M
New York Light, 10th Battery
Pennsylvania Light, Batteries E and F
4th U.S. Artillery, Battery F

Cavalry Division (Brig. Gen. Alfred Pleasonton)
1st Brigade (Maj. Charles J. Whiting)
5th U.S. Cavalry
6th U.S. Cavalry

2d Brigade (Col. John F. Farnsworth)
8th Illinois Cavalry
3d Indiana Cavalry
1st Massachusetts Cavalry
8th Pennsylvania Cavalry

3d Brigade (Col. Richard H. Rush)
4th Pennsylvania Cavalry
6th Pennsylvania Cavalry

4th Brigade (Col. Andrew T. McReynolds)
1st New York Cavalry
12th Pennsylvania Cavalry

5th Brigade (Col. Benjamin F. Davis)
8th New York Cavalry
3d Pennsylvania Cavalry

Artillery
2d U.S. Artillery, Batteries A, B, L, and M
3d U.S. Artillery, Batteries C and G

Unassigned
1st Maine Cavalry (on detached duty)
15th Pennsylvania Cavalry (Detachment)

Army of Northern Virginia, Confederate States Army
General Robert E. Lee

Longstreet's Command (Maj. Gen. James Longstreet)[7]
McLaws' Division (Maj. Gen. Lafayette McLaws)
Kershaw's Brigade (Brig. Gen. J. B. Kershaw)
2d South Carolina Infantry
3d South Carolina Infantry
7th South Carolina Infantry
8th South Carolina Infantry

Cobb's Brigade (Brig. Gen. Howell Cobb)
16th Georgia Infantry
24th Georgia Infantry
Cobb's (Georgia) *Legion*
15th North Carolina Infantry

Semmes' Brigade (Brig. Gen. Paul J. Semmes)
10th Georgia Infantry
53d Georgia Infantry
15th Virginia Infantry
32d Virginia Infantry

Barksdale's Brigade (Brig. Gen. William Barksdale)
13th Mississippi Infantry
17th Mississippi Infantry
18th Mississippi Infantry
21st Mississippi Infantry

---

[7] Organized on 14 March 1862 as *Longstreet's* command, it officially became the *I Corps* on 6 November. *OR*, pp. 698–99.

Artillery (*Maj. S. P. Hamilton*)
  Manly's (North Carolina) *Battery*
  Pulaski (Georgia) *Artillery*
  Richmond (Fayette) *Artillery*
  Richmond Howitzers, 1st Company
  Troup (Georgia) *Artillery*

Anderson's Division (*Maj. Gen. Richard H. Anderson*)
  Wilcox's Brigade (*Col. Alfred Cumming*)
    8th Alabama Infantry
    9th Alabama Infantry
    10th Alabama Infantry
    11th Alabama Infantry

  Mahone's Brigade (*Col. William A. Parham*)
    6th Virginia Infantry
    12th Virginia Infantry
    16th Virginia Infantry
    41st Virginia Infantry
    61st Virginia Infantry

  Featherston's Brigade (*Brig. Gen. Winfield S. Featherston*)
    12th Mississippi Infantry
    16th Mississippi Infantry
    19th Mississippi Infantry
    2d Mississippi Battalion

  Armistead's Brigade (*Brig. Gen. Lewis A. Armistead*)
    9th Virginia Infantry
    14th Virginia Infantry
    38th Virginia Infantry
    53d Virginia Infantry
    57th Virginia Infantry

  Pryor's Brigade (*Brig. Gen. Roger A. Pryor*)
    14th Alabama Infantry
    2d Florida Infantry
    8th Florida Infantry
    3d Virginia Infantry

  Wright's Brigade (*Brig. Gen. A. R. Wright*)
    44th Alabama Infantry
    3d Georgia Infantry
    22d Georgia Infantry
    48th Georgia Infantry

Artillery (*Maj. John S. Saunders*)
    Donaldsonville (Louisiana) *Artillery*
    Huger's (Virginia) *Battery*
    Moorman's (Virginia) *Battery*
    Thompson's (Grimes') (Virginia) Battery

Jones' Division (Brig. Gen. David R. Jones)
    Toombs' Brigade (Brig. Gen. Robert Toombs)
        2d Georgia Infantry
        15th Georgia Infantry
        17th Georgia Infantry
        20th Georgia Infantry

    Drayton's Brigade (Brig. Gen. Thomas F. Drayton)
        50th Georgia Infantry
        51st Georgia Infantry
        15th South Carolina Infantry

    Pickett's Brigade (Col. Eppa Hunton)
        8th Virginia Infantry
        18th Virginia Infantry
        19th Virginia Infantry
        28th Virginia Infantry
        56th Virginia Infantry

    Kemper's Brigade (Brig. Gen. J. L. Kemper)
        1st Virginia Infantry
        7th Virginia Infantry
        11th Virginia Infantry
        17th Virginia Infantry
        24th Virginia Infantry

    Jenkins' Brigade (Col. Joseph Walker)
        1st South Carolina Infantry
        2d South Carolina Rifles
        5th South Carolina Infantry
        6th South Carolina Infantry
        4th South Carolina Battalion
        Palmetto (South Carolina) *Sharpshooters*

    Anderson's Brigade (Col. George T. Anderson)
        1st Georgia Infantry (Regulars)
        7th Georgia Infantry
        8th Georgia Infantry
        9th Georgia Infantry
        11th Georgia Infantry

Artillery
> Fauquier (Virginia) Artillery*
> Loudoun Virginia) Artillery*
> Turner (Virginia) Artillery*
> Wise (Virginia) Artillery
> *On detached duty.

Walker's Division (Brig. Gen. John G. Walker)
> Walker's Brigade (Col. Van H. Manning)
>> 3d Arkansas Infantry
>> 27th North Carolina Infantry
>> 46th North Carolina Infantry
>> 48th North Carolina Infantry
>> 30th Virginia Infantry
>> French's (Virginia) Battery

> Ransom's Brigade (Brig. Gen. Robert Ransom, Jr.)
>> 24th North Carolina Infantry
>> 25th North Carolina Infantry
>> 35th North Carolina Infantry
>> 49th North Carolina Infantry
>> Branch's Field Artillery (Virginia)

Hood's Division (Brig. Gen. John B. Hood)
> Hood's Brigade (Col. W. T. Wofford)
>> 18th Georgia Infantry
>> Hampton (South Carolina) Legion
>> 1st Texas Infantry
>> 4th Texas Infantry
>> 5th Texas Infantry

> Law's Brigade (Col. E. M. Law)
>> 4th Alabama Infantry
>> 2d Mississippi Infantry
>> 11th Mississippi Infantry
>> 6th North Carolina Infantry

Artillery (Maj. B. W. Forbel)
> German (South Carolina) Artillery
> Palmetto (South Carolina) Artillery
> Rowan (North Carolina) Artillery

Evans' Brigade (Brig. Gen. Nathan G. Evans)
> 17th South Carolina Infantry
> 18th South Carolina Infantry
> 22d South Carolina Infantry

23d South Carolina Infantry
Holcombe (South Carolina) *Legion*
Macbeth (South Carolina) *Artillery*

Artillery
Washington (Louisiana) *Battalion (Col. J. B. Walton)* (4 companies)

Lee's Battalion (Col. S. D. Lee)
Ashland (Virginia) *Artillery*
Bedford (Virginia) *Artillery*
Brooks' (South Carolina) *Artillery*
Eubanks' (Virginia) *Artillery*
Madison (Louisiana) *Artillery*
Parker's (Virginia) *Battery*

Jackson's Command (Maj. Gen. Thomas J. Jackson)[8]
Ewell's Division (Brig. Gen. A. R. Lawton)
Lawton's Brigade (Col. M. Douglass)
13th Georgia Infantry
26th Georgia Infantry
31st Georgia Infantry
38th Georgia Infantry
60th Georgia Infantry
61st Georgia Infantry

Early's Brigade (Brig. Gen. Jubal A. Early)
13th Virginia Infantry
25th Virginia Infantry
31st Virginia Infantry
44th Virginia Infantry
49th Virginia Infantry
52d Virginia Infantry
58th Virginia Infantry

Trimble's Brigade (Col. James A. Walker)
15th Alabama Infantry
12th Georgia Infantry
21st Georgia Infantry
21st North Carolina Infantry
1st North Carolina Battalion (attached to
21st North Carolina Infantry)

---

[8] Organized as *Jackson*'s command on 14 March 1862, it officially became the *II Corps* on 6 November.

Hay's Brigade (Brig. Gen. Harry T. Hays)
   5th Louisiana Infantry
   6th Louisiana Infantry
   7th Louisiana Infantry
   8th Louisiana Infantry
   14th Louisiana Infantry

Artillery (*Maj. A. R. Courtney*)
   Charlottesville (Virginia) *Artillery**
   Chesapeake (Maryland) *Artillery**
   Courtney (Virginia) *Artillery**
   Johnson's (Virginia) *Battery*
   Louisiana Guard Artillery
   1st Maryland Battery*
   Staunton (Virginia) *Artillery**
   *On detached duty.

Hill's Light Division (Maj. Gen. Ambrose P. Hill)
   Branch's Brigade (Brig. Gen. L. O'B. Branch)
      7th North Carolina Infantry
      18th North Carolina Infantry
      28th North Carolina Infantry
      33d North Carolina Infantry
      37th North Carolina Infantry

   Gregg's Brigade (Brig. Gen. Maxcy Gregg)
      1st South Carolina Infantry (Provisional Army)
      1st South Carolina Rifles
      12th South Carolina Infantry
      13th South Carolina Infantry
      14th South Carolina Infantry

   Field's Brigade (Colonel J. M. Brockenbrough)
      40th Virginia Infantry
      47th Virginia Infantry
      55th Virginia Infantry
      22d Virginia Battalion

   Archer's Brigade (Brig. Gen. J. J. Archer)
      5th Alabama Battalion
      19th Georgia Infantry
      1st Tennessee Infantry (Provisional Army)
      7th Tennessee Infantry
      14th Tennessee Infantry

Pender's Brigade (Brig. Gen. William D. Pender)
    16th North Carolina Infantry
    22d North Carolina Infantry
    34th North Carolina Infantry
    38th North Carolina Infantry

Thomas' Brigade (Col. Edward L. Thomas)
    14th Georgia Infantry
    35th Georgia Infantry
    45th Georgia Infantry
    49th Georgia Infantry

Artillery (*Maj. R. L. Walker*)
    Branch (North Carolina) *Artillery**
    Crenshaw's (Virginia) *Battery*
    Fredericksburg (Virginia) *Artillery*
    Letcher (Virginia) *Artillery**
    Middlesex (Virginia) *Artillery**
    Pee Dee (South Carolina) *Artillery*
    Purcell (Virginia) *Artillery*
    *On detached duty.

Jackson's Division (Brig. Gen. John R. Jones)
    Winder's Brigade (Col. A. J. Grigsby)
        2d Virginia Infantry
        4th Virginia Infantry
        5th Virginia Infantry
        27th Virginia Infantry
        33d Virginia Infantry

Taliaferro's Brigade (Col. E. T. H. Warren)
    47th Alabama Infantry
    48th Alabama Infantry
    10th Virginia Infantry
    23d Virginia Infantry
    37th Virginia Infantry

Jones' Brigade (Col. B. T. Johnson)
    21st Virginia Infantry
    42d Virginia Infantry
    48th Virginia Infantry
    1st Virginia Battalion

Starke's Brigade (Brig. Gen. William E. Starke)
    1st Louisiana Infantry
    2d Louisiana Infantry
    9th Louisiana Infantry

10th Louisiana Infantry
15th Louisiana Infantry
Coppens' (Louisiana) Battalion

Artillery (Maj. L. M. Shumaker)
Alleghany (Virginia) Artillery
Brockenbrough's (Maryland) Battery
Danville (Virginia) Artillery
Hampden (Virginia) Artillery
Lee (Virginia) Battery
Rockbridge (Virginia) Artillery

Hill's Division (Maj. Gen. Daniel H. Hill)
Ripley's Brigade (Brig. Gen. Roswell S. Ripley)
4th Georgia Infantry
44th Georgia Infantry
1st North Carolina Infantry
3d North Carolina Infantry

Rodes' Brigade (Brig. Gen. R. E. Rodes)
3d Alabama Infantry
5th Alabama Infantry
6th Alabama Infantry
12th Alabama Infantry
26th Alabama Infantry

Garland's Brigade (Brig. Gen. Samuel Garland, Jr.)
5th North Carolina Infantry
12th North Carolina Infantry
13th North Carolina Infantry
20th North Carolina Infantry
23d North Carolina Infantry

Anderson's Brigade (Brig. Gen. George B. Anderson)
2d North Carolina Infantry
4th North Carolina Infantry
14th North Carolina Infantry
30th North Carolina Infantry

Colquitt's Brigade (Col. A. H. Colquitt)
13th Alabama Infantry
6th Georgia Infantry
23d Georgia Infantry
27th Georgia Infantry
28th Georgia Infantry

Artillery (*Major Pierson*)
    Hardaway (Alabama) *Battery*
    Jeff. Davis (Alabama) *Artillery*
    Jones' (Virginia) *Battery*
    King William (Virginia) *Artillery*

Reserve Artillery (*Brig. Gen. William N. Pendleton*)
    Brown's Battalion (*Col. J. Thompson Brown*)
        Powatan Artillery
        Richmond Howitzer, 2d and 3d Companies
        Salem Artillery
        Williamsburg Artillery

    Cutts' Battalion (*Lt. Col. A. S. Cutts*)
        Blackshears' (Georgia) *Battery*
        Irwin (Georgia) *Artillery*
        Lloyd's (North Carolina) *Battery*
        Patterson's (Georgia) *Battery*
        Ross' (Georgia) *Battery*

    Jones' Battalion (*Maj. H. P. Jones*)
        Morris (Virginia) *Artillery*
        Orange (Virginia) *Artillery*
        Turner's (Virginia) *Artillery*
        Wimbish's (Virginia) *Battery*

    Nelson's Battalion (*Maj. William Nelson*)
        Amherst (Virginia) *Artillery*
        Fluvanna (Virginia) *Artillery*
        Huckstep's (Virginia) *Battery*
        Johnson's (Virginia) *Battery*
        Milledge (Georgia) *Artillery*

    Miscellaneous Artillery
        Cutshaw's (Virginia) *Battery*
        Dixie (Virginia) *Artillery*
        Magruder (Virginia) *Artillery*
        Rice's (Virginia) *Battery*
        Thomas (Virginia) *Artillery* (on detached duty)

Cavalry (*Maj. Gen. James E. B. Stuart*)
    Hampton's Brigade (*Brig. Gen. Wade Hampton*)
        1st North Carolina Cavalry
        2d South Carolina Cavalry
        10th Virginia Cavalry
        Cobb's (Georgia) *Legion*
        Jeff. Davis Legion

Lee's Brigade (Brig. Gen. Fitzhugh Lee)
  1st Virginia Cavalry
  3d Virginia Cavalry
  4th Virginia Cavalry
  5th Virginia Cavalry
  9th Virginia Cavalry

Robertson's Brigade (Brig. Gen. B. H. Robertson)
  2d Virginia Cavalry
  6th Virginia Cavalry
  7th Virginia Cavalry
  12th Virginia Cavalry
  17th Virginia Battalion

Horse Artillery (Capt. John Pelham)
  Chew's (Virginia) *Battery*
  Hart's (South Carolina) *Battery*
  Pelham's (Virginia) *Battery*

CASUALTIES

Estimates of numbers engaged in Civil War battles vary; statistics on killed, wounded, captured, and missing are incomplete. The reports of casualties at the Battle of Antietam shown in the official records are certainly inaccurate. Often these reports are qualified by "about," "not over," or "less than." In addition, they do not show numbers of wounded who later died or the missing who later returned to duty or had been captured. The casualty estimates shown below are drawn from reports in the *Official Records,* submitted one to several months after the battle. While Union reports show casualty statistics for 17 September 1862, Confederate reports show the total number of killed and wounded for the Maryland Campaign, including the battles of South Mountain, Harper's Ferry, Sharpsburg (Antietam), and Shepherdstown (Boteler's Ford). Confederate cavalry casualties are not shown. *Stuart's* cavalry brigades spent 17 September guarding the flanks of the Confederate Army, thus their casualties were relatively few.

TABLE 1: ARMY OF THE POTOMAC, CASUALTIES DURING THE BATTLE OF ANTIETAM, 17 SEPTEMBER 1862

Unit	Killed Ofcrs	Killed Men	Wounded Ofcrs	Wounded Men	Missing Ofcrs	Missing Men	Aggregate
I Corps	25	392	100	1,951	0	122	2,590
II Corps	63	820	188	3,671	3	393	5,138
V Corps	1	16	2	88	0	2	109
VI Corps	8	63	22	313	2	31	439
IX Corps	24	414	98	1,698	2	113	2,349
XII Corps	17	258	63	1,323	0	85	1,746
Cavalry Division	1	6	0	23	0	0	30
Total	139	1,969	473	9,067	7	746	12,401

TABLE 2: *ARMY OF NORTHERN VIRGINIA*, CASUALTIES DURING THE
MARYLAND CAMPAIGN, 14–19 SEPTEMBER 1862

Unit	Killed	Wounded	Aggregate
Longstreet's Command			
McLaws' Division	205	1,256	1,461
R. H. Anderson's Division	134	887	1,021
D. R. Jones' Division	142	818	960
Walker's Division	177	144	321
Hood's Division	133	830	963
Evans' Brigade*	47	262	309
Subtotal	838	4,197	5,035
Jackson's Command			
Ewell's Division	161	854	1,015
A. P. Hill's Division	113	818	931
Jackson's Division	111	435	546
D. H. Hill's Division	451	1,735	2,186
Subtotal	836	3,842	4,678
Total	1,674	8,039	9,713

*This brigade was not assigned to a division but operated with *Longstreet's* command.

Source: U.S. War Department, *The War of the Rebellion: A Compilation of the Official Records of the Union and Confederate Armies,* 70 vols. (Washington, D.C.: Government Printing Office, 1893), ser. 1, vol. 19, pt. 1, pp. 189–200, 810–11, 843, 860–62, 888, 906–07.

ORGANIZATION

In the Eastern Theater of the war, in September 1862 the principal adversaries were the Union Army of the Potomac and the Confederate *Army of Northern Virginia*. The Union Army was organized into six infantry corps and one cavalry division. Artillery was organized into batteries of four to six guns each, with two or more batteries assigned to each of the army's eighteen divisions. The total strength of the Army of the Potomac during the Battle of Antietam was approximately 85,000 men.

In September 1862 the *Army of Northern Virginia* consisted of two infantry "commands" comprising a total of nine infantry divisions and one cavalry division. (The formation of corps was not authorized in the Confederate Army until after the Battle of Antietam.) Artillery batteries were assigned to each of the army's divisions and to the army's reserve artillery. At the time of the Battle of Antietam, the strength of the *Army of Northern Virginia* was about 60,000, though only about 40,000 actually participated.

For Civil War armies the infantry regiment was the basic administrative and tactical unit. Regimental headquarters consisted of a colonel, lieutenant colonel, major, adjutant, quartermaster, surgeon (a major), two assistant surgeons, a chaplain, sergeant major, quartermaster sergeant, commissary sergeant, hospital steward, and two principal musicians. Each company was generally staffed by a captain, a first lieutenant, a second lieutenant, sometimes a third lieutenant, a first sergeant, 4 sergeants, 8 corporals, 2 musicians, and 1 wagoner.

The authorized strength of a Civil War infantry regiment was about 1,000 officers and men arranged in ten companies plus a headquarters and (at least for of the first half of the war) a band. Discharges for physical disability, disease, special assignments (as bakers, hospital nurses, or wagoners), courts-martial, and battle injuries all combined to reduce effective combat strength. Before long a typical regiment might be reduced to fewer than 500 troops.

Brigades were made up of two or more regiments, with four regiments being most common. Union brigades averaged 1,000 to 1,500 infantry, while Confederate brigades averaged 1,500 to 1,800. Union brigades were designated by a number within their division, while Confederate brigades were designated by the name of a current or former commander. Divisions were formed of two or more brigades. Union divisions contained 2,500 to 4,000 infantrymen, while Confederate infantry divisions were somewhat larger, containing 5,000 to 6,000 men.

A corps was formed of two or more divisions. Two or more corps constituted an army, the largest operational organization.

TACTICS

The tactical legacy of the eighteenth century emphasized close-order formations of soldiers trained to maneuver in concert and fire by volleys. These "linear" tactics stressed the tactical offensive. Assault troops advanced in line, two ranks deep, with cadenced steps, stopping to fire volleys on command and finally rushing the last few yards to pierce the enemy line with a bayonet charge. These tactics were adequate for troops armed with single-shot, muzzle-loading, smoothbore muskets with an effective range of roughly eighty yards. The close-order formation was necessary to concentrate the firepower of these inaccurate weapons. Bayonet charges had a chance of success because infantry could rush the last eighty yards before the defending infantrymen could reload their muskets.

The U.S. Army's transition from smoothbore to rifled muskets in the mid-nineteenth century had two main effects in the American Civil War: it strengthened the tactical defensive and increased the number of casualties in the attacking force. With weapons that could cause casualties out to 1,000 yards, defenders firing rifles could decimate infantry formations attacking according to linear tactics.

During the Civil War the widespread use of the rifle often caused infantry assault formations to loosen somewhat, with individual soldiers seeking available cover and concealment. However, because officers needed to maintain visual and verbal control of their commands during the noise, smoke, and chaos of combat, close-order tactics to some degree continued to the end of the war.

The smallest tactical unit employed individually on the battlefield was a brigade, usually consisting of four regiments. Units generally moved on roads or cross-country in column formation, four men abreast. Upon reaching the battlefield, each regiment was typically formed into a line two ranks deep, each man's shoulders touching the shoulders of the men next to him. Regulations prescribed the distance between the ranks as thirteen inches. Both front and rear ranks were capable of firing either by volley or individually. Two paces behind the rear rank was an open rank of "file closers," selected noncommissioned officers charged with preventing straggling and desertion. During a battle each regiment might send forward two companies in extended skirmish order, keep six companies in its main line, and hold two in the rear as a reserve. As the fighting progressed, additional companies might be fed into the skirmish line or the skirmishers might regroup on the main line. A regiment of 500 men might have a front almost 200 yards wide.

SMALL ARMS

In 1855 the U.S. Army adopted a .58-caliber rifled musket to replace the .69-caliber smoothbore. The new infantry weapon was muzzle loaded, its rifled barrel taking a hollow-based cylindroconical bullet slightly smaller than the diameter of the bore. The loading procedure required the soldier to withdraw a paper cartridge containing powder and bullet from his cartridge box, tear open one end of the cartridge with his teeth, pour the powder into the muzzle, place the bullet in the muzzle, and ram it to the breech using a metal ramrod. The soldier then placed a copper percussion cap on a hollow cone at the breech. To fire the weapon, he cocked the hammer; when he pulled the trigger, the hammer struck the cap and ignited the powder charge in the breech. Each soldier was expected to be capable of loading and firing three aimed shots per minute. Although the maximum range of a rifled musket was sometimes over 1,000 yards, actual fields of fire were often very short, with musketry relying on volume at close range rather than accuracy at long range.

The basic ammunition load for each infantry soldier was forty rounds in the cartridge box. When more action was expected, twenty additional rounds were issued to each soldier, who placed them in his uniform pockets or knapsack. In addition, 100 rounds per man were held in the brigade or division trains and another 100 rounds in the corps trains.

At the beginning of the war, a shortage of rifled muskets on both sides forced the Northern and Southern governments to issue the older smoothbore weapons and purchase weapons from European nations. As the war progressed, more soldiers were armed with rifled weapons; though late in the war some troops on both sides still carried smoothbores.

Officers generally carried both single- and multiple-shot handguns. The types of handguns used by both sides were innumerable; however, two of the most common were six-shot revolvers produced by Colt and Remington, in both .36- and .44-caliber.

The Union cavalry was initially armed with sabers and handguns but soon added breech-loading carbines. In addition to Sharps and Spencer carbines, dozens of other types of breechloaders, from .52- to .56-caliber, were issued. Confederate cavalrymen might be armed with a wide variety of handguns, shotguns, muzzle-loading carbines, or captured Federal weapons.

TABLE 3: TYPICAL CIVIL WAR SMALL ARMS

Weapon	Effective Range (in yards)	Theoretical Rate of Fire (in rounds/minute)
U.S. rifled musket, Muzzle loaded, .58-caliber	400–600	3
English Enfield rifled musket, Muzzle loaded, .577-caliber	400–600	3
Smoothbore musket, Muzzle loaded, .69-caliber	100–200	3

Source: Ernest F. Fisher, Jr., "Weapons and Equipment Evolution and Its Influence Upon the Organization and Tactics in the American Army, 1775–1963," Unpubl Ms, Office of the Chief of Military History, 1963, File 2–3.7, AB.Z, U.S. Army Center of Military History (CMH), Washington, D.C.

ARTILLERY

At the Battle of Antietam, the Army of the Potomac had an estimated 293 guns, of which 166 were rifled. Although Antietam Creek physically separated many Union guns from the battlefield proper, many guns east of the creek could fire on Confederate positions along Hagerstown Pike. On the morning of 17 September approximately ninety Union guns were operating on the west side of the creek, mostly on the Union right flank north of Dunker Church. More guns were sent to the battlefield during the day, and by evening there were approximately 162 Union guns west of Antietam Creek.

On 17 September the *Army of Northern Virginia* had an estimated 246 guns, of which 82 were rifled, 112 smoothbore, and 52 of unknown type. The Confederates reported having captured 73 guns at Harper's Ferry on 15 September, but none were assembled into batteries in time to be used in the Battle of Antietam.

The artillery of both armies was generally organized into batteries of four or six guns. Regulations prescribed a captain as battery commander, while lieutenants commanded two-gun "sections." Each gun made up a platoon, under a sergeant ("chief of the piece") with eight crewmen and six drivers.

For transport, each gun was attached to a two-wheeled cart, known as a limber and drawn by a six-horse team. The limber chest carried thirty to fifty rounds of ammunition, depending on the size of guns in the battery. In addition to the limbers, each gun had at least one caisson, also drawn by a six-horse team. The caisson carried additional ammunition in two chests, as well as a spare wheel and tools. A horse-drawn forge and a battery wagon with tools accompanied each battery. A battery at full regulation strength included all officers, noncommissioned officers, buglers, drivers, cannoneers, and other specialized functions and might exceed 100 officers and men. With spare horses included, a typical six-gun battery might have 100–150 horses.

A battery could unlimber and fire an initial volley in about one minute, and each gun could continue firing two aimed shots a minute. A battery could "limber up" in about one minute as well. The battery practiced "direct fire": the target was in view of the gun. The prescribed distance between guns was fourteen yards from hub to hub. Therefore, a six-gun battery would represent a front of about 100 yards. Depth of the battery position from the gun muzzle, passing the limber, to the rear of the caisson was prescribed as forty-seven yards. In practice, these measurements might be altered by terrain.

During the firing sequence cannoneers took their positions as in the diagram below. At the command "Commence firing," the gunner ordered "Load." While the gunner sighted the piece, Number 1 sponged the bore; Number 5 received a round from Number 7 at the limber and carried the round to Number 2, who placed it in the bore. Number 1 rammed the round to the breech, while Number 3 placed a thumb over the vent to prevent premature detonation of the charge. When the gun was loaded and sighted, Number 3 inserted a vent pick into the vent and punctured the cartridge bag. Number 4 attached a lanyard to a friction primer and inserted the primer into the vent. At the command "Fire," Number 4 yanked the lanyard. Number 6 cut the fuses, if necessary. The process was repeated until the command to cease firing was given.

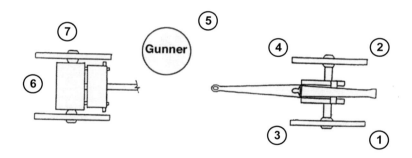

Table 4: Typical Civil War Field Artillery

Weapon	Tube Composition	Tube Length (in inches)	Effective Range at 5° Elevation (in yards)
6-pdr. Model 1841 Smoothbore field gun 3.67-in. dia. bore	Bronze	60	1,523
12-pdr. "Napoleon" Smoothbore gun-howitzer 4.62-in. dia. bore	Bronze	59	1,680
10-pdr. Parrott rifle 2.9-in. dia. bore	Cast iron	78	1,950
3-in. Ordnance rifle 3.0-in. dia. bore	Wrought iron	73	1,835
20-pdr. Parrott rifle 6.67-in. dia. bore	Cast iron	89	2,100

Note: Cannon were generally identified by the weight of their solid iron round shot; though some, like the 3-inch ordnance rifle, used the diameter of the bore for identification.

Sources: Henry L. Abbott, *Siege Artillery in the Campaigns against Richmond with Notes on the 15-inch Gun*, Professional Papers 14 (Washington, D.C.: Government Printing Office, 1867); Alfred Mordecai, *Artillery for the United States Land Service as Devised and Arranged by the Ordnance Board, Including Drawings and Tables of Dimensions of the Ordnance for the Land Service of the United States, 1841* (Washington, D.C.: J. & G. S. Gideon, 1849); *Instruction for Field Artillery, Prepared by a Board of Artillery Officers* (Philadelphia: J. B. Lippincott, 1863); Rpt, Joseph M. Hanson, 27 May 1940, sub: A Report on the Deployment of the Artillery at the Battle of Antietam, Md., With a View To Making Battery Positions at the Antietam National Battlefield Site, in National Park Service Files, Antietam National Battlefield.

Artillery Projectiles

Civil War field artillery employed four basic types of projectiles: solid shot for long-range accuracy, shells for medium-range blast, case shot for medium-range fragmentation, and canister for close-range defense.

Shot   *Bolt*

Solid Projectiles

Round (spherical) projectiles of solid iron for smoothbores were commonly called cannonballs, or shot. When elongated for rifled weapons, the projectile was known as a bolt. Solid projectiles were used against opposing batteries, wagons, buildings, etc., as well as enemy personnel. While shot could ricochet across open ground against advancing infantry or cavalry, bolts tended to bury themselves upon impact with the ground and therefore were not used a great deal by field artillery.

Spherical Shell   *Rifled Shell*

Shell

The shell, whether spherical or conical, was a hollow iron projectile filled with a black powder–bursting charge. It would typically break into five to ten large fragments. Spherical shells were exploded by fuses set into an opening in the shell, which ignited the shell near the intended target. The time of detonation was determined by adjusting the length of the fuse. Rifled shells were detonated by similar-timed fuses or by a percussion fuse detonating the shell upon impact.

Spherical Case Shot

Rifled Case Shot

Case Shot

Case shot had a thinner wall than a shell and was filled with a number of smaller lead or iron balls (eighty for a 12-pounder). A timed fuse ignited a small bursting charge inside the shell, which fragmented the casing and scattered the contents into the air. Case shot was intended to burst fifty to seventy-five yards short of the target, the fragments being carried forward by the velocity of the shot.

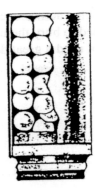

Canister

Canister

Canister consisted of a tin cylinder filled with iron balls tightly packed in sawdust, which turned the cannon into a giant shotgun. Canister was an extremely effective antipersonnel weapon, with a maximum range of 350 yards. In emergencies, double loads of canister could be used at ranges less than 200 yards with a single propelling charge.

LOGISTICS

U.S. Army Bureau System

Bureau chiefs and heads of staff departments were responsible for various aspects of the Army's administration and logistics and reported directly to the Secretary of War. The division of responsibility and authority over them among the Secretary of War, the Assistant Secretaries, and the General in Chief was never specified. The supply departments functioned independently and without effective coordination throughout most of the Civil War, though much improved after Grant took command.

Logistical support was entrusted to the heads of four supply departments in Washington: the Quartermaster General, responsible for clothing and equipment, forage, animals, transportation, and housing; the Commissary General for rations; the Chief of Ordnance for weapons, ammunition, and miscellaneous related equipment; and the Surgeon General for medical supplies, evacuation, treatment, and hospitalization of the wounded.

For other support there were the Adjutant General, the Inspector General, the Paymaster General, the Judge Advocate General, the Chief of Engineers, and the Chief of Topographical Engineers.

The military department was the basic organizational unit for administrative and logistical purposes, and the commander of each department controlled the support in that area with no intervening level between his departmental headquarters and the bureau chiefs in Washington. There were six departments when the war started (East, West, Texas, New Mexico, Utah, and Pacific); however, later on, boundaries changed and several geographical departments might be grouped together as a military "division" headquarters.

Army depots were located in major cities: Boston, New York, Baltimore, Washington, Cincinnati, Louisville, St. Louis, Chicago, New Orleans, and San Francisco. Philadelphia was the chief depot and manufacturing center for clothing. Advanced and temporary supply bases were established as needed to support active operations. Until 1864 most depots were authorized the rank of captain as commander, who despite his low rank and meager pay had tremendous resources of men, money, and materiel under his control. There were a few exceptions, notably Col. Daniel H. Rucker at the Washington Quartermaster Depot and Col. George D. Ramsay at the Washington Arsenal. The primary function of the depots was to procure supplies and prepare them for use in the field by repacking, assembling, or other similar tasks.

Procurement was decentralized. Purchases were made on the market by low-bid contract in the major cities and producing areas by depot officers. Flour and some other commodities were procured closer to the troops when possible. Cattle were contracted for at specific points, and major beef depots were maintained at Washington (on the grounds of the unfinished Washington Monument); Alexandria, Virginia; and Louisville, Kentucky. The Subsistence Department developed a highly effective system of moving cattle on the hoof to the immediate rear of the armies in the field to be slaughtered by brigade butchers and issued to the troops the day before consumption.

The Confederate Army used a similar system with depots at Richmond; Staunton; Raleigh; Atlanta; Columbus, Georgia; Huntsville; Montgomery; Jackson, Mississippi; Little Rock; Alexandria, Louisiana; and San Antonio.

Supply Operations

Most unit logistics was accomplished at the regimental level. The regimental quartermaster was normally a line lieutenant designated by the regimental commander. His duties included submitting requisitions for all quartermaster supplies and transport; accounting for regimental property including tents, camp equipment, extra clothing, wagons, forage, and animals; issuing supplies; and managing the regimental trains. The regimental commissary officer, also designated from the line, requisitioned, accounted for, and issued rations. The regimental ordnance officer had similar duties regarding arms and ammunition and managed the movement of the unit ammunition train.

In theory, logistical staff positions above the regiment were filled by a fully qualified officer of the supply department concerned. However, experienced officers were in perpetual short supply: many authorized positions were filled by officers and noncommissioned officers from the line units or left vacant with the duties performed by someone in addition to his own. This problem existed in both armies, where inexperience and ignorance of logistical principles and procedures generally reduced levels of support.

The Soldier's Load: About 45 lbs. (Union)—musket and bayonet (14 lbs.); 60 rounds; 3–8 days' rations; canteen, blanket, or overcoat; shelter half; ground sheet; mess gear (cup, knife, fork, spoon, and skillet); personal items (sewing kit, razor, letters, Bible, etc.). Confederates usually had less, about 30 lbs.

Official U.S. Ration: 20 oz. fresh or salted beef or 12 oz. pork or bacon; 18 oz. flour or 20 oz. cornmeal (bread in lieu if possible); 1.6 oz. rice, .64 oz. beans, or 1.5 oz. dried potatoes; 1.6 oz. coffee or .24 oz. tea; 2.4 oz. sugar; .54 oz. salt; and .32 gill vinegar.

Union Marching Ration: 16 oz. "hardtack," 12 oz. salt pork, or 4 oz. fresh meat; 1 oz. coffee; 3 oz. sugar; and salt.

Confederate Ration: Basically the same but with slightly more sugar and less meat, coffee, vinegar, and salt and seldom issued in full. For the *Army of Northern Virginia* usually half of meat issued and coffee available only when captured or exchanged through the lines for sugar and tobacco. During the Maryland Campaign foraging was disappointing, so Confederate soldiers supplemented the issue ration with corn from the fields and fruit from the orchards.

Forage: Each horse required 14 lbs. hay and 12 lbs. grain per day; mules needed the same amount of hay and 9 lbs. grain. No other item was so bulky and difficult to transport.

Union Annual Clothing Issue: 2 caps, 1 hat, 2 dress coats, 3 pr. trousers, 3 flannel shirts, 3 flannel drawers, 4 pr. stockings, and 4 pr. bootees (high-top shoes). Artillerymen and cavalrymen were issued jackets and boots instead of bootees. Allowance = $42.

Confederate: Officially, the Confederate soldier was almost equally well clothed; but the Quartermaster was seldom able to supply the required items and soldiers wore whatever came to hand, the home-dyed butternut jackets and trousers being characteristic items. Shortages of shoes were a constant problem.

Tents: The Sibley (tepee) held 20 men, feet to center pole; early in the war, the Union introduced the *tent de' Abri* (shelter half) used by the French Army and called "dog" tent by witty soldiers—now called pup tent.

Baggage: Enlisted men of both armies were required to carry their own. Union order of September 1862 limited officers to blankets, one small valise or carpet bag, and an ordinary mess kit. Confederate standards allowed generals 80 lbs., field officers 65 lbs., and captains and subalterns 50 lbs.

Wagons: The Union's standard 6-mule Army wagon could haul 4,000 lbs. on good roads in the best of conditions but seldom exceeded 2,000 (with 4 mules 1,800 lbs.) at a rate of 12–24 miles a day. Confederates often used 4-mule wagons with smaller capacity.

The Army of the Potomac authorized wagons as follows:

Corps headquarters.   4
Division and brigade headquarters.   3
Regiment of infantry   6
Artillery battery and cavalry   3

One wagon per regiment was reserved for hospital stores and one for grain for officers' horses.

The *Army of Northern Virginia* used 4-mule wagons as follows:

Division headquarters   3
Brigade headquarters   2
Regiment headquarters.   1
Regiment's medical stores   1
Regiment's ammunition   1
Per 100 men for baggage,
    camp equipment, rations, etc..   1

Numbers of supply wagons per 1,000 men:

Army of the Potomac (1862)   29
Jackson in the Valley (1862)   7
Army of Northern Virginia (1863)   28
Army of the Potomac (1864)   36
Sherman's March to the Sea (1864)   40
Napoleon's standard 12.5

SELECTED BIOGRAPHICAL SKETCHES

Union Officers

George B. McClellan
1826–1885, Pennsylvania

McClellan was born in Phil-adelphia to a family that moved within the upper ranks of local society. He attended private schools before entering West Point, where in 1846 he gradu-ated second in a class of fifty-nine. Assigned to the Corps of Engineers, McClellan par-ticipated in the Mexican War, where he was awarded brevets of 1st lieutenant and captain. After the war he served briefly as an instructor at West Point. As a member of a board of offi-cers, McClellan went abroad to observe the Crimean War and study European armies.

George B. McClellan

In 1857 McClellan resigned his army commission to become chief engineer of the Illinois Central Railroad. Five years later, when the Civil War broke out, he was president of the Ohio and Mississippi Railroad. McClellan entered the war as a major gen-eral of volunteers and was soon commissioned with the same rank in the Regular Army. His success in a minor victory at Rich Mountain, West Virginia, just ten days before the Union disaster at First Bull Run, brought him to the public eye at a critical time. He was assigned command of the army at Washington (later known as the Army of the Potomac) and in November became general in chief of the Army, replacing Winfield Scott.

In the spring of 1862 the "Young Napoleon" took the Army of the Potomac by water to the Virginia Peninsula to capture Richmond. His departure as field commander resulted in his be-ing relieved of command as general in chief on 11 March. During the Peninsula Campaign McClellan greatly overestimated the number of Confederates defending their capital and constantly asked the government for additional men in order to advance. Unable to provide the thousands of men requested, the War Department in early August ordered McClellan to withdraw his army from the peninsula. The Army of the Potomac was to unite with the Army of Virginia under Maj. Gen. John Pope. In late August, however, before all of McClellan's forces could join with Pope, the Army of Virginia was defeated at Second Bull Run. The remnants of Pope's command were then consolidated with the Army of the Potomac.

In early September *Lee* crossed the Potomac River into Maryland, and McClellan was tasked with leading the reorganized Army of the Potomac north. He confronted the Confederates along Antietam Creek near Sharpsburg. On 17 September the two armies fought to a draw in the Battle of Antietam, and two days later *Lee* withdrew back to Virginia. McClellan failed to pursue the Confederates and remained on the battlefield until early November, reorganizing his command and requesting reinforcements. This delay prompted his dismissal as army commander; although he still retained his commission as major general, he held no further command during the war. After running unsuccessfully for president in 1864 (and resigning his commission on Election Day), McClellan and his family sailed to Europe, not returning for three-and-a-half years. McClellan served as governor of New Jersey from 1878–1881.

Ambrose E. Burnside
1824–1881, Indiana

Born to a poor family of Quakers, Burnside was indentured at an early age as a tailor's apprentice. Afterward he entered West Point and graduated in the class of 1847, during the Mexican War. Although sent to Mexico, he did not arrive until the war had ended. Burnside was then ordered to duty in New Mexico, where he was wounded in an engagement with Apaches. During duty in New Mexico, Burnside found the cavalry carbine unsuited for plains service and

Ambrose E. Burnside

invented the Burnside breechloading rifle. In 1852 he resigned his commission and settled in Rhode Island to manufacture the new rifle, hoping for a lucrative government contract. After failing to obtain a contract, he was forced to turn over the patent rights to creditors. Still in debt, Burnside found employment with his former West Point classmate George McClellan at the Illinois Central Railroad in Chicago.

By 1860 Burnside was the company treasurer with an office in New York City. At the beginning of the Civil War, Burnside returned to Rhode Island to take command of a regiment of militia, which led to Washington in April 1861. At the Battle of First Bull Run on 21 July, Burnside was a colonel in command of a brigade and by early August had been promoted to brigadier general of volunteers. In early 1862 Burnside commanded an expedition against the North Carolina coast, where his troops captured Roanoke Island, New Berne, Beaufort, and Fort Macon. For these accomplishments he was promoted to major general in March 1862. In July Burnside's troops, plus troops from other commands, were organized into the IX Corps. During the Second Bull Run Campaign the IX Corps was attached to Pope's Army of Virginia, although Burnside himself remained near Fredericksburg. During the Maryland Campaign Burnside was briefly assigned command of a wing, which consisted of the I and IX Corps, in McClellan's army.

Burnside had twice before been offered command of the Army of the Potomac, after the Peninsula and Second Bull Run Campaigns. Each time he had expressed that he did not feel competent to command such a large force. However, in early November President Lincoln relieved McClellan and Burnside reluctantly accepted the command. A month later he crossed his army to the south of the Rappahannock River but was defeated at the Battle of Fredericksburg on 13 December.

In January 1863 Burnside attempted to launch another offensive campaign, known as the Mud March; poor weather conditions resulted in another failure. President Lincoln relieved him of command and transferred him to the Western Theater. While he was commander of the Department of the Ohio, his forces occupied East Tennessee and captured Knoxville. In 1864 Burnside was ordered back east, once again commanding the IX Corps, and participated in Grant's overland campaign in Virginia. He led his corps through the Battles of the Wilderness, Spotsylvania, and Cold Harbor and the operations against Petersburg. After the failed attack at the Battle of the Crater at Petersburg in July, Maj. Gen. George G. Meade charged Burnside with disobedience of orders. A court of inquiry found Burnside "answerable for the want of success," and in April 1865 he resigned from the Army. After the war Burnside was three-time governor of Rhode Island; from 1875 until his death, he served as a U.S. Senator.

Joseph Hooker
1814–1879, Massachusetts

Joseph Hooker

Hooker graduated from West Point in 1837 and served in the Mexican War, rising to the rank of captain of artillery. After a leave of absence from 1851–1853, he resigned his commission to take up farming in California. When the Civil War broke out in 1861, Hooker was made brigadier general of volunteers and commanded troops defending Washington. He was assigned command of a division in the Army of the Potomac during the Peninsula Campaign in early 1862 and promoted to major general of volunteers in May. During the Battle of Second Bull Run in late August, Hooker's division was attached to Pope's Army of Virginia. In the reorganization of the army at the beginning of the Maryland Campaign in September, Hooker was assigned command of the I Corps, Army of the Potomac, which he led in the Battle of Antietam on 17 September. Soon afterward he was promoted to brigadier general in the Regular Army. At the Battle of Fredericksburg on 13 December, Hooker served as a "grand division" commander of the Army of the Potomac, commanding the III and V Corps. In January 1863 he was assigned command of the Army of the Potomac and led that force to defeat at the Battle of Chancellorsville, 1–4 May 1863. When *Lee* advanced into Pennsylvania in June, Hooker followed. In late June, after the War Department refused his request for additional troops from the garrison at Harper's Ferry, Hooker asked to be relieved of the army command—his request was immediately accepted. In September Hooker was transferred to the Western Theater, where he commanded the XI and XII Corps (later consolidated into the XX Corps). In July 1864, when one of Hooker's subordinates was promoted over him, Hooker was relieved at his own request. For the remainder of the war he was assigned various departmental commands. Hooker remained on active duty until 1868, when he was retired for disability contracted in the line of duty.

Edwin V. Sumner
1797–1863, Massachusetts

Born in Boston, Sumner enlisted in the Regular Army in 1819 as a 2d lieutenant of infantry. He served in the Black Hawk War, became captain of the 2d Dragoons in 1833, and was employed on the Western Frontier. In 1838 he was placed in command of the school of cavalry practice at Carlisle, Pennsylvania. Sumner was promoted to major in 1846 and served in the Mexican War. In 1855 he was promoted to colonel of the 1st Cavalry. Three years later he was in command of the Department of the West. With

Edwin V. Sumner

the outbreak of the Civil War, Sumner was appointed a brigadier general in the Regular Army and sent to command the Department of the Pacific. He was recalled in 1862 to take command of the I Corps, Army of the Potomac. His command participated in the Peninsula Campaign during the summer of 1862, and he was wounded twice. After being appointed major general of volunteers, Sumner entered the Maryland Campaign in command of a wing consisting of the II and XII Corps. At the Battle of Antietam on 17 September, Sumner personally led a division of the II Corps into battle; it was driven off the field and Sumner was wounded. At the Battle of Fredericksburg on 13 December, Sumner commanded the Right Grand Division, containing the II and IX Corps. Although Sumner was ordered to remain at his headquarters during the battle, his command participated in the unsuccessful attacks against the Confederate defense on Marye's Heights. Upon the accession of Hooker to command of the Army of the Potomac in January 1863, Sumner requested a transfer to the Western Theater. On the way to take command of the Department of the Missouri, he died in New York of natural causes.

Joseph K. F. Mansfield
1803–1862, Connecticut

Mansfield graduated from West Point in 1822, standing second in a class of forty. He was assigned to the Corps of Engineers and for the next three years planned fortifications for the defense of the harbors and cities on the East Coast. In 1832 he was promoted to 1st lieutenant and in 1838 to captain. Mansfield served in the Mexican War as chief engineer under Maj. Gen. Zachary Taylor. During the war Mansfield received brevets of major and lieutenant colonel for gallant and meritorious conduct. He was appointed inspector general of the U.S. Army in 1853 with the rank of colonel and at the beginning of the Civil War was commissioned brigadier general of volunteers and placed in command of the Department of Washington and the city of Washington. Mansfield was in command of Newport News in late 1861 and was engaged in the capture of Norfolk and Suffolk, Virginia, the following spring. On 18 July he was promoted to major general of volunteers. During the Maryland Campaign in September Mansfield was assigned command of Maj. Gen. Nathaniel P. Banks' XII Corps after Banks was detailed to duty in Washington. Mansfield had been in command only three days when at the Battle of Antietam he was mortally wounded while mistakenly riding between the opposing lines. He died the following morning.

Joseph K. F. Mansfield

Robert E. Lee
1807–1870, Virginia

Robert E. Lee

Lee, a member of a promi-
nent Virginia family, was the
son of "Light Horse Harry" Lee,
a hero of the American Revolu-
tion. His older brother, Sydney
Lee, served as commandant
at Annapolis, commanded
Commodore Perry's flagship
in the Japan expedition, and
later served in the Confederate
Navy. Robert graduated from
West Point in 1829, second in
his class of forty-six. He then
served at various forts along
the east coast before being assigned chief engineer for the
St. Louis, Missouri, harbor.
During the Mexican War *Lee*
served on the staff of General Winfield Scott in the Vera Cruz
expedition, receiving in succession the brevets of major, lieutenant colonel, and colonel. After the war *Lee* returned to supervise
construction of fortifications until appointed superintendent
of West Point, a position he held from 1852 to 1855. Later he
was transferred from the engineer corps and assigned as lieutenant colonel of the 2d Cavalry. In late 1859 the abolitionist
John Brown made his raid on the U.S. arsenal at Harper's Ferry;
Lee, on leave in Washington, was sent with a force of marines
from the Navy Yard to capture the raiders. In early 1861 *Lee* was
promoted to colonel of the 1st Cavalry, his commission signed
by the newly elected Abraham Lincoln. However, when he was
offered command of forces that would invade the South, *Lee*
resigned his commission.

In late April he was appointed major general and commander
of Virginia military forces. A month later, when Virginia became
part of the Confederacy, *Lee* was commissioned first a brigadier
general in the Confederate Army (no higher rank having been
created at that time) and later general. In March 1862 he became
the military adviser to *President Jefferson Davis*. At the beginning
of June *Lee* succeeded the wounded *General Joseph E. Johnston* in

command of the *Army of Northern Virginia* in charge of defending Richmond. *Lee* led his army through a series of victories—at the Battles of the Seven Days, Second Bull Run, Fredericksburg, and Chancellorsville—punctuated by reverses at Antietam and Gettysburg. In February 1865 *Lee* was appointed general in chief of the Confederate armies; but two months later, on 9 April, he was forced to surrender the *Army of Northern Virginia* at Appomattox Court House. After the war *Lee* accepted the presidency of Washington College at Lexington, Virginia, and served there until his death. (The school's name was later changed to Washington and Lee University.)

James Longstreet
1821–1904, South Carolina

James Longstreet

At the age of ten *Longstreet* moved to Alabama with his parents. He graduated from the U.S. Military Academy at West Point in 1842 and served in the Mexican War, during which he was severely wounded and also brevetted as a major. He was promoted to captain in 1852 and to major and paymaster in 1858 and stationed at Albuquerque, New Mexico. Resigning his commission in 1861, *Longstreet* was commissioned a brigadier general in the Confederate Army and ordered to report to Manassas, where he commanded a brigade. On 18 July his command repulsed a Federal attack at Blackburn's Ford; during the Battle of First Bull Run on 21 July, it threatened the Federal rear. In October he was promoted to major general and given command of a division under *General Johnston*. During the summer of 1862 he commanded the right wing of the Confederate army before Richmond in the Battle of Seven Pines. He commanded his own and *Maj. Gen. A. P. Hill*'s divisions under *Lee* in the successful Battles of Gaines' Mill and Frayser's Farm. Afterward he commanded a wing of *Lee's Army of Northern Virginia*. At Second Bull Run, 30–31 August 1862, *Longstreet*'s wing was instrumental in crushing Pope's army and driving it back to

Washington. In the Maryland Campaign his command fought at South Mountain on 14 September and in the Battle of Antietam on 17 September.

In October *Longstreet* was promoted to lieutenant general and his wing was redesignated the I Corps. The I Corps was responsible for the successful defense of Marye's Heights in the Battle of Fredericksburg on 13 December. In 1862 *Longstreet* suffered a personal tragedy when three of his four children died in Richmond of scarlet fever. In the spring of 1863 *Longstreet* operated with part of his corps at Suffolk, Virginia, missing the Battle of Chancellorsville, 1–6 May; but he soon rejoined *Lee* at Fredericksburg. The Gettysburg Campaign found *Longstreet's* corps moving into Pennsylvania, and he personally reached the field at Gettysburg on the afternoon of 1 July. On 2 July *Hood's* and *McLaws'* divisions of *Longstreet's* corps (*Maj. Gen. George E. Pickett's* division having not yet arrived), made an unsuccessful attempt to turn the Federal left. *Pickett's* division arrived by 3 July and, reinforced by commands from *A. P. Hill's* corps, unsuccessfully attempted to break the Federal center. After *Lee's* army had retired to Virginia, *Longstreet*, with *Hood's* and *McLaws'* divisions, was sent to reinforce *General Braxton Bragg* in northern Georgia, where *Longstreet*, as a commander of the left wing at Chickamauga, crushed the Federal right. Rejoining the *Army of Northern Virginia* in time for Grant's 1864 Overland Campaign, *Longstreet's* command participated in the Battle of the Wilderness, where on 6 May he was wounded accidentally by his own men. After returning to duty *Longstreet* commanded a portion of the defense of Richmond, and his command later joined the retreat at Appomattox. After the war *Longstreet* settled in New Orleans and became a member of the Republican Party, much to the chagrin of his former Confederate comrades. President Grant appointed him surveyor of customs, and *Longstreet* served as U.S. marshal of Georgia and minister to Turkey.

Thomas J. Jackson
1824–1863, Virginia

Jackson was born in what is now Clarksburg, West Virginia. His parents died while he was still a child, and he was raised by an uncle. At the age of eighteen he was appointed to West Point and graduated in 1846 in time to participate in the Mexican War. He was assigned to the 1st Regular Artillery and participated in the storming of Chapultepec. In 1851 he resigned his Army commission and accepted a teaching position at the Virginia Military Institute in Lexington, Virginia. For ten years he was a professor of natural philosophy and

Thomas J. Jackson

an instructor of artillery tactics. While at the Institute, *Jackson* married Elinor Junkin; after her death a year later he took a leave of absence from the Institute and spent the summer of 1856 in Europe. After his return to Virginia, *Jackson* was married again, to Mary Anna Morrison of North Carolina. Upon the outbreak of the Civil War, *Jackson* was commissioned a colonel in the Virginia forces and sent to Harper's Ferry, where he was active in organizing recruits. *Jackson* was soon appointed brigadier general and given command of a brigade in the Army of the Shenandoah. The brigade participated in the Battle of First Bull Run on 21 July, in which *Jackson* and his command received the nickname Stonewall. A month later *Jackson* was promoted to major general. In November he was assigned command of the Valley District, consisting of the Stonewall Brigade and other attached troops. In May 1862 he began his celebrated Valley Campaign, winning victories at McDowell, Front Royal, Winchester, Cross Keys, and Port Republic. *Jackson* then marched to Richmond to join *Lee's Army of Northern Virginia* in the defense of the capital. After the Peninsula Campaign, *Jackson*, commanding a wing of *Lee's Army of Northern Virginia*, was detached and sent on a flanking march around the Union army under Pope. *Jackson* captured Pope's supply base at Manassas and, after being joined by *Lee* and the remainder of the Confederate Army, defeated Pope at the Battle of Second Bull Run on 30–31 August. In the Maryland Campaign, *Jackson*'s wing captured the 11,000-man Union garrison at Harper's Ferry and then joined *Lee* at Sharpsburg to participate in the Battle of Antietam on 17 September. Two months later he was promoted to lieutenant general and his wing officially became the II Corps. At the Battle of Fredericksburg on 13 December, *Jackson*'s corps held the right flank of *Lee*'s army and easily repelled half-hearted Union assaults. The following year, at the Battle of Chancellorsville, he led his corps on a wide flank march on 2 May that routed the Union XII Corps. Personally reconnoitering the front lines that night, *Jackson* was shot accidentally by his own men. Following the amputation of his arm, he died eight days later, on 10 May 1863.

James E. B. Stuart
1833–1864, Virginia

James E. B. Stuart

After graduating from West Point in 1854, *Stuart* spent much of his service with the 1st Cavalry in Kansas. Following Virginia's secession, *Stuart* resigned his commission and became a captain of cavalry in the Confederate Army. He participated in the Battle of First Bull Run in July 1861 and afterward was promoted to brigadier general. In June 1862 he conducted the first of his celebrated cavalry raids, riding completely around McClellan's army on the Virginia peninsula. *Stuart* was promoted to major general in July and given command of all cavalry of the *Army of Northern Virginia*. After another bold and successful raid in August, this time to John Pope's rear, *Stuart* covered the last stage of *Stonewall Jackson*'s flanking movement before the Battle of Second Bull Run, 30–31 August. He was actively engaged in the subsequent Maryland Campaign and the Battle of Antietam on 17 September. After the latter battle, *Stuart* again rode around the Union army, ranging as far as southern Pennsylvania and capturing over a thousand horses. He participated in the Battle of Fredericksburg in December and, at the Battle of Chancellorsville in May 1863, provided security for *Jackson*'s flank attack. When *Jackson* was wounded, *Stuart* took temporary command of *Jackson*'s corps. In June 1863 *Stuart*'s command fought in the largest cavalry battle of the war at Brandy Station, where he was surprised by Union cavalry under Brig. Gen. Alfred Pleasonton. The approach of Confederate infantry forced Pleasonton's cavalry to withdraw across the Rappahannock. In the Gettysburg Campaign, *Stuart* was absent until the evening of 2 July, after having ridden too far east of *Lee*'s army. Without *Stuart* to provide him with information, *Lee* did not learn soon enough of the Union concentration north of the Potomac, which resulted in the Battle of Gettysburg. In the spring of 1864 *Stuart*'s command, now decreased in size and deficient in equipment, engaged a force of Union cavalry at the Battle of Yellow Tavern on 11 May. During the engagement *Stuart* was mortally wounded and died the following day.

SUGGESTED STOPS

Stop 1: North Woods. At dawn on 17 September 1862, elements of Maj. Gen. Joseph Hooker's I Corps advanced from their bivouacs north of the Joseph Poffenberger home, southward through the North Woods, toward the D. R. Miller farmhouse. Brig. Gen. James B. Ricketts' division advanced on the East Woods, and Brig. Gen. Abner Doubleday's division advanced south toward the Cornfield and West Woods. Two of Brig. Gen. George G. Meade's three brigades were between those of Ricketts and Doubleday and slightly to the rear, while the third brigade held the southern edge of the East Woods. Hooker's advance occurred under small-arms fire from skirmishers at the Miller farm and artillery fire from *Col. S. D. Lee*'s batteries near Dunker Church to the south and from *Capt. John Pelham*'s batteries on Nicodemus Hill to the west. Throughout the morning the North Woods was held and used by Union forces as a staging area for the intense fighting to the south. In the late morning the North Woods became a refuge for the surviving elements and wounded of the I and II Corps returning from the fighting in the Cornfield and West Woods.

Stop 2: East Woods. On the morning of 17 September Brig. Gen. Truman Seymour's brigade of Meade's division held the southern edge of the East Woods, having skirmished with men of *Brig. Gen. John B. Hood*'s command the night previous. Ricketts' three brigades advanced south along Smoketown Road, led by the brigade of Brig. Gen. Abram Duryea. The brigades of Brig. Gen. George L. Hartsuff and Col. William A. Christian were to advance in close support of Duryea. A shell fragment wounded Hartsuff, and his brigade failed to advance. Christian's brigade was halted temporarily in the East Woods after Christian lost his nerve and left the battlefield. Hartsuff's and Christian's brigades, under new commanders, finally emerged from the East Woods; but Duryea's brigade had already been driven back. By 0730 the Confederates still occupied the southern edge of the East Woods when Maj. Gen. Joseph K. F. Mansfield's XII Corps attacked down Smoketown Road. Mansfield led the corps himself and was mortally wounded. By roughly 0900 the Confederates, finally forced from the East Woods by the XII Corps, fell back to Dunker Church and the West Woods. Maj. Gen. George

S. Greene's division of the XII Corps pushed south along Smoketown Road and halted on the ridge opposite the West Woods and Dunker Church. Around 1300 Maj. Gen. William B. Franklin's VI Corps arrived at the East Woods. Except for an aborted attempt by a portion of Maj. Gen. William F. Smith's division to occupy the West Woods, the VI Corps remained in reserve during the battle.

Stop 3: Cornfield. The thirty-acre Miller Cornfield would become known after the battle as the Bloody Cornfield or simply the Cornfield. While *Maj. Gen. Thomas J. Jackson's* main line of defense formed a line 300 yards farther south, *Brig. Gen. A. R. Lawton* had sent a strong force into the standing corn itself. Hooker's advance reached the Cornfield around 0600, with Doubleday's division striking the western portion and Ricketts' brigades entering from the East Woods. For more than an hour the fighting raged as *Jackson* fed reinforcements into the Cornfield. Doubleday's and Rickett's divisions, joined by Meade's reserves, finally drove the Confederates from the Cornfield and pushed south toward Dunker Church. Around 0700 *Jackson* launched a counterattack with *Hood's* division, supported by a portion of *Maj. Gen. Daniel H. Hill's* command. The Confederates drove the Union troops back to the northern edge of the Cornfield but were halted by the pointblank fire of Union guns near the Miller home and from the East Woods. Upon the arrival of the XII Corps, the Confederates withdrew from the Cornfield to the relative safety of the West Woods. Around 0900 Maj. Gen. John Sedgwick's division of Maj. Gen. Edwin V. Sumner's II Corps advanced to the East Woods, then across the Cornfield and into the West Woods. There, the division was attacked in flank and driven back across the Cornfield. *Jackson* attempted to follow Sedgwick's retreating division but was halted by Union artillery north of the Cornfield and near the East Woods. For all practical purposes, the fighting in the Cornfield was finished.

Stop 4: West Woods. After learning that Hooker had been wounded and that his corps had suffered a large number of casualties, McClellan sent Sedgwick's division of the II Corps across the Antietam. Sedgwick's three brigades entered the East Woods and then marched through the Cornfield toward the West Woods. Sumner led the division in person. When the column reached Hagerstown Pike, it came under sharp artillery fire from *Maj. Gen. James E. B. Stuart's* guns, planted beyond the woods on high ground to the west. The brigade of Brig. Gen. Willis A. Gorman, followed by that of Brig. Gen. Napolean J. T. Dana, entered the West Woods and halted. There is some question whether Brig. Gen. Oliver O. Howard's brigade actually entered the woods. Seeing the approach of Sedgwick's division, *Jackson* sent word to *Brig. Gen. Jubal A. Early* (who had been sent with his brigade to support *Stuart*) to return and take command of *Ewell's Division* in place of *Lawton*, who had been disabled. Presently, other Confederate reinforcements began to arrive. The divisions of *Brig. Gen. John G. Walker* and *Maj. Gen. Lafayette McLaws* and the brigade of *Col. George T. Anderson* moved to the right and left of *Early*, concealed by the West Woods. Portions of Sedgwick's division entered the woods, but their stay was brief. Almost a dozen Confederate brigades struck the flanks of Sedgwick's three brigades, and in about twenty minutes Sedgwick's division was decimated and driven out of the West Woods. Within those twenty minutes, nearly 2,000 of Sedgwick's men were killed or wounded.

Stop 5: Sunken Road. The Sunken Road marks the site of the Confederate center at Antietam. It is the remnant of an old farm land that connected Hagerstown Pike with Boonsboro Pike. Brig. Gen. William H. French's division of Sumner's II Corps crossed the Antietam behind Sedgwick's division. After halting briefly near the East Woods, French's troops moved south across the Mumma and Roulette farms and struck *D. H. Hill's* division in the Sunken Road around 0900. *Brig. Gen. A. R. Wright's* and *Posey's* brigades of *R. H. Anderson's* division arrived from Harper's Ferry and reinforced the Confederate line. After almost two hours Maj. Gen. Israel B. Richardson's division of Sumner's II Corps arrived on the left of French's command. The Confederates continued to hold the road until a misunderstanding by a Confederate officer caused a portion of *Hill's* left to withdraw. At the same time, Richardson's men broke through the right. The Sunken Road was taken, but the Union victors were briefly flanked when two regiments of *Walker's* command drove Greene's division from the high ground near the present-day location of the Visitor Center. The arrival of a VI Corps brigade drove the Confederates back across Hagerstown Pike and into the West Woods.

Stop 6: Burnside Bridge. Around 0900 Maj. Gen. Ambrose E. Burnside's IX Corps was ordered to cross this bridge. Defending the bridge were some 400 Georgians of *Brig. Gen. Robert Toombs'* brigade. For four hours the Confederates blocked several Union attempts, until the 51st Pennsylvania and 51st New York Infantries were able to rush across. Meanwhile, Brig. Gen. Isaac P. Rodman's division had crossed the creek at Snavely's Ford, nearly a mile to the south, while several companies from the

28th Ohio Infantry of the Kanawha Division crossed at a ford a few hundred yards above the bridge. After the Union crossing at, above, and below the bridge, *Toombs'* men fell back up the slope to the edge of Sharpsburg. Around 1500, after crossing over most of his command, Burnside advanced the IX Corps up the slope toward the town, threatening to cut off the Confederate line of retreat to the Potomac River. Around 1600 a portion of *A. P. Hill's* division arrived from Harper's Ferry and, after striking the left flank of the IX Corps, drove Burnside's troops back to the heights just above the bridge.

Stop 7: National Cemetery. In March 1865 the State of Maryland established a burial site on the Antietam battlefield for the men who died in the Maryland Campaign. The cemetery was dedicated on 17 September 1867, the fifth anniversary of the battle. The original plan allowed for burial of soldiers from both sides, but it was later changed to inter only the Union dead there. Confederate remains were re-interred in private cemeteries in Hagerstown and Mt. Olivet, Maryland, and in Shepherdstown, West Virginia. Approximately 2,800 Southerners, over 60 percent of them unknown, are buried in these three cemeteries.

There are 4,776 Union remains (1,836 unknown) buried in the National Cemetery from the Battles of Antietam, South Mountain, Monocacy, and other actions in Maryland. All the unknowns are marked with small square stones. These stones contain the grave number; on some graves, a small second number represents how many unknowns are buried in that grave. A few of the larger, traditional stones also mark unknown graves.

In addition, more than 200 non–Civil War dead are buried here. Veterans and their wives from the Spanish-American War, World Wars I and II, and the Korean War were buried here until the cemetery closed in 1953. An exception to the closure was made for the burial of Keedysville resident Patrick Howard Roy, U.S. Navy. Firemen Roy, killed during the terrorist attack on the USS *Cole*, was buried in the cemetery on 29 October 2000.

The large statue of the private soldier in the center of the cemetery, known locally as Old Simon, was erected on 17 September 1880.

MAP SYMBOLS

VEGETATION

	Orchard
	Woods
	Stubble
	Corn
	Pasture
	Plowed Fields
	Unknown

GENERAL SYMBOLS

	Buildings
	Church
	Major Road
	Minor Road

MILITARY SYMBOLS

Confederate	Union	
		Units of various strength
		Cavalry of various strength
		Axis of Advance
		Axis of Retreat
		Skirmish Line
		Artillery

Note: The topographic contour lines on the maps in this publication are based on the 1899 *Map of the Battlefield of Antietam,* prepared under the direction of the Antietam Battlefield Board and drawn by Charles H. Ourand. The Ourand map used a local datum point on the Antietam battlefield—the water level at Burnside Bridge—and sets that contour at 0 feet. That point is 375 feet above sea level. The maps are adjusted accordingly, and the contour intervals are based on 25 feet rather than the conventional 10 feet.

NOTES

NOTES